T0271169

Protests and the Media

This insightful volume critically explores activist events in their scale and their capacity to attract media attention through a critical event studies lens, offering new perspectives on protests and social movement.

This book conceives events of dissent as the public manifestation of counter-narratives that articulate advocacy for policy change. It focuses on the material and virtual manifestation of protest events and the media response to them, associated with three active social movements – Reclaim These Streets, Extinction Rebellion, and Black Lives Matter. In doing so, the text sheds light on how different political orientations within the media articulate the representation of events of dissent manifest by these groups, and how this results in significantly different opinion-forming statements on the issues behind those movements, as well as how this reflects mediated assessment of the responses of politicians, the public, and emergency service responses to protest events. Furthermore, it will explore the role of the Internet in the organisation of protest events and their part in the formation of networks of resistance, enabling the roll out of events with a global reach – demonstrated, more recently, by protests across many European cities against the war in Ukraine.

This timely and significant book will appeal to scholars of and those interested in event tourism, protest, political communication, and media, among others.

Giedre Kubiliute was drawn to Event Management studies due to her belief that events can be emotive and transformative experiences. Giedre grew up in Lithuania at the time of The Singing Revolution, The Baltic Way, and The January Events, which formed her view of protests and dissent as crucial catalysts for positive societal change. Recent world events presented a perfect opportunity to follow her passion and align her studies with further research into the subject of protests.

Ian R. Lamond is Senior Lecturer in Events at Leeds Beckett University, Leeds, United Kingdom. His research interests include the conceptual foundations of critical event studies, creative forms of dissent, critical spatiality in social and cultural theory, and events that mark the end of life.

Routledge Critical Event Studies Research Series
Editors
Rebecca Finkel
Queen Margaret University, UK
David McGillivray
University of the West of Scotland, UK

For more information about this series, please visit: *www.routledge.com/Routledge-Critical-Event-Studies-Research-Series/book-series/RCE*

Protests and the Media

A Critical Event Studies Exploration into the Future of Protest

Giedre Kubiliute and Ian R. Lamond

Routledge
Taylor & Francis Group

LONDON AND NEW YORK

First published 2024
by Routledge
4 Park Square, Milton Park, Abingdon, Oxon OX14 4RN

and by Routledge
605 Third Avenue, New York, NY 10158

Routledge is an imprint of the Taylor & Francis Group, an informa business

British Library Cataloguing-in-Publication Data
A catalogue record for this book is available from the British Library

ISBN: 978-1-032-60821-1 (hbk)
ISBN: 978-1-032-60824-2 (pbk)
ISBN: 978-1-003-46064-0 (ebk)

DOI: 10.4324/9781003460640

Typeset in Times New Roman
by Apex CoVantage, LLC

Contents

Protest and media
A CES perspective

Introduction

Towards the end of 2022, Collins declared that the *Word of the Year* was Permacrisis which is defined, on its website, as: 'an *extended* period of *instability* and insecurity, esp (sic) one resulting from a *series* of catastrophic *events*'[1] (collinsdictionary.com, 2022, n.p.). The manifestations of living through a time of permacrisis are many and varied. Along with ongoing concerns associated with issues such as the rise and rise of hate crime (Home Office, 2023), climate change, the conflict in the Ukraine, possible new COVID variants, and the cost-of-living, our present state of precarity encompasses a growing scrutiny of protest, events of dissent, the actions of trade unions, and social movements. Such a state of continuous precarity and anxiety contributes to daily life manifesting as what could be construed as a *perma*-liminal space – a Turner-esque continuous realm of being in a nowhere space that is betwixt and between (Turner, 2017 [1969]).

While it has been argued that the liminal's opening up of multiple alternative outcomes provides a creative space for experimentation, whether that be within events, leisure, and tourism (see, e.g. Pielichaty, 2015; Rodríguez-Campo et al., 2021) or organisational management (such as discussed in Howard-Grenville, 2011, and Söderland & Borg, 2018), these constructions concentrate on a liminal phase understood as a short-term disruption. The *perma*-liminal represents an ongoing sphere of uncertainty, where points of settlement are sought but are always, already, in a process of moving on. As such, the realm of daily life becomes one ungraspable without any recourse to contestation (Bringel & Domingues, 2015) and conflictuality (Touraine, 2000). We are all touched by it – whether we are standing on a picket line or waiting for a medical procedure; queuing in a food bank, worrying about how the next bill will be paid; or deeply troubled by how technological advances may make a role, one that has been instrumental in establishing our understanding of our identity, obsolete.

Research into protest offers us one route into reflecting on our current condition of permacrisis – of *perma*-liminality. However, much research into social movements has tended to gravitate towards their organisation,

DOI: 10.4324/9781003460640-1

formation, and effectiveness (Diani & Mische, 2015) with little attention to how protest is articulated through the material and virtual events which constitute their protest action (Feigenbaum et al., 2013; della Porta, 2008). With their interest in examining points of contestation and conflict, protest events offer a rich area for inquiry within the field of critical event studies (CES). Aligned with this are issues associated with how events of dissent also raise important questions linked to how they are made manifest through, and represented within, diverse media platforms (Gerbaudo, 2012; Jones, 2019).

Despite this being a global phenomenon, within the UK, this has been particularly apparent in several high-profile protest actions by social movements such as Black Lives Matter; Reclaim These Streets, and Extinction Rebellion (XR) and in a significant upsurge in unionised industrial action: the UK saw the highest number of days lost to labour disputes in 2022/2023 for more than a decade (ONS, 2023). Interest in research associated with social movements is growing. There are an increasing number of event scholars interested in researching protests as events (Smith, 2015; Duric et al., 2022). In addition, there are also a growing number of academics, across the wider social sciences, who are interested in exploring protest from an evental perspective (Rovisco & Ong, 2016; Wagner-Pacifici, 2017; Gubernat & Rammelt, 2017).

In this book, we will investigate the mediated representation of events of dissent and protest through an interrogation of key aspects of events manifest by social movements in mainstream media, the impact of that mediation on activists and their activism, and how those movements have negotiated and managed their use of various media platforms as a means of articulating dissent. Before we commence, it is important to lay out some of the conceptual ground within which our discussion will be located. First, we shall consider what critical event studies (henceforth CES) is. From this, we shall consider an approach to investigating events of dissent through an association between CES and the Advocacy Coalition Framework (hereafter ACF) as developed by Sabatier and Weible (2007). In doing so, we will gain an insight into why the study of protest is of particular interest to CES research. That discussion will lead us into our third theme – a consideration of *actant* in Latour's actor–network theory (ANT), the critical (relational) geography of Doreen Massy, and the affirmative ethics of Rosi Braidotti. This will draw us to a conclusion around the axiological, ontological, and epistemic perspective we will be adopting within the remainder of the book.

Finally, we will conclude our introduction with an outline of the structure of the book, outlining the key issues and concerns in each of its remaining chapters.

What is CES?

There are many routes into establishing a response to this question, and it would be unnecessarily overwhelming to attempt to summarise these here.

Instead, we will begin with setting out one of the basic first steps in the process of establishing a critical approach to the study of events and build up a workable picture of CES from that.

As suggested by Spracklen and Lamond (2016), the first significant difference between *critical event studies* and *event studies* is the problematisation of the referent of *event*. Getz, in his seminal work on establishing the field of event studies, defines its remit as 'the academic field devoted to creating knowledge and theory about planned events' (Getz & Page, 2020, p. 3). It 'draws from a large number of foundation disciplines and closely related professional fields . . . to better understand why [events] exist and how we can manage them better' (Ibid, p. 4). This is unpacked further through drawing on Pernecky (2016), whose foundational definition of event studies is expressed as 'whatever researchers invested in the study of events do' (p. 4).

While this second definition is closer to CES than that of Getz, it still nests the study of events within the 'three important discourse on events – event management, event tourism, and the impacts of events on society' (Getz & Page,2020, p. 4). That is both definitions assume an ontological status for the referent of *event* that CES does not. By problematising *event,* the term loses any ontic roots, and, as such, it cannot form part of anything that can be simply articulated in the form *x is an event.*

While we may indicate manifestations of *events* – the Eurovision Song Contest, the Olympic Games, the fall of the Berlin Wall, the horrendous atrocities of Auschwitz, the death of Queen Elizabeth II, a mass shooting at a gay club in the United States, or discovering the milk for your morning coffee has gone off – these are all confluences of multiple ruptures and disruptions. Each has been drawn together to form a narrative, an *evental* landscape, one of many bounded but possible narratives, which can be disseminated, shared, articulated, re-articulated, etc., in multiple ways.

Event is rupture and multiplicity – if that is acknowledged then event studies becomes a post-disciplinary attitude that draws on one or more narratives associated with a given evental landscape and to interrogate some aspect(s) of the discursive multiplicity made apparent through those ruptures. Where it becomes *critical* is when its intense interest in how and for what purpose, identity, power, domination, repression, othering, etc., that the exposed contested and conflictual narratives, expressed through those landscapes, become manifest.

The consequences of such a perspective are far reaching – going beyond those 'three important discourse on events' that Getz and Page (2020, p. 4) refer to, which I mentioned earlier. CES is an attitude, an orientation, that draws from and – importantly – feeds into many social sciences, humanities, post-humanities, and physical sciences. To unpack this further, here, it would consume far too much space, though we will suggest some aspects of that unpacking through the next two sections.

CES and ACF – the significance of protest

If we are to consider protest, events of dissent, from a CES perspective, then it is important that we consider how it is to be conceptualised within that arena. As we have argued elsewhere (Lamond, 2019), one of the simplest ways of understanding protest is as a manifestation of a policy declaration – either for policy change or for the maintenance of an existing policy that is perceived to be in jeopardy. It is because of this, that seeking approaches from policy process studies would seem to be a reasonable step.

ACF was initially developed by Paul Sabatier as a means of grasping the nuance and complexity of the policy process. According to Sabatier (1988), ACF moves away from previous frameworks that tended to focus on either heuristic recommendations for best practice in policy decision-making (top-down models) or evaluative toolkits for assessing the effective implementation of policy change and how that can inform future policy planning decision-making (bottom-up approaches). While the framework relies on a series of core concepts, it has continued to adapt and evolve through its application to, and interrogation of, practice. So, what are those core concepts?

Central to ACF is the idea that pressures to address a policy position occur when there is a systemic shock to a prevailing or dominant system, what CES would refer to as a rupture or disruption to an evental landscape. Those *shocks* could be within a regime (government, economy, culture, organisation, etc.) or external to it. Scale can also be varied – from a global climate catastrophe to someone being attacked on the way home from work or something as apparently innocuous as the missing of an appointment. What the shock does is move a situation from one of stability to one of contestation. The apprehension of it, and how it is articulated, will be bounded by such things as the sociocultural climate, individual and institutional resilience, and where it sits within cycles of change and renewal.

Weible et al. (2011) and Jenkins-Smith et al. (2014) suggest that coalitions form quickly around different responses to the emerging situation. It is the conflictualities between these coalitions, which produce the contestation that occurs around the systemic shock. Those coalitions are articulated through formal and informal communicative channels, which can encompass heated institutionalised debates and casual conversations in the pub. Individual attachment to a coalition's orientation may not be conscious, and the association with a coalition can be fluid, with some actors migrating between different coalitional positions. The likelihood of migration reflects the epistemic community of which they are a part (the community, or communities, of practice of which they are a part – Meijerink, 2005) and their world view (their degree of cohesion to the ontology suggested by the coalition's response to the shock – Matti & Sandstrom, 2013). As the shock remains unresolved, or unacceptably addressed, the epistemic and ontic bonds holding it together will be tested, resulting in those less tightly bonded to the coalition migrating to different positions.

Events of dissent and protest are both the manifestation of a fuzzy set (Zadeh, 1965) of coalitional positions that bear a family resemblance (Wittgenstein, 2009 [1953]) to each other and further system shock(s) that carry the potential of drawing, sustaining, or repelling further coalitional membership. Those further shocks may include the presentation of new information not previously available or accessible to members of a coalition, the material response to an event of protest (such as on-site public/police/military action), or how that event is mediated through various media platforms.

It is the very public nature of protest, its manifestation of contestation and conflictuality in the public realm (materially or digitally), that makes events of dissent particularly interesting to interrogate through the lens of critical event studies. However, if we wish to dig deeper into understanding protest events, we need to move beyond ACF and try to unpack both the cohesion and ephemerality of these coalitions, one that recognises that the bonds associated with social movements, and campaign activities attached to action for social justice, are ethico-political as well as epistemic and ontic (i.e. they also have an axiological perspective). To do that, we would argue, moves us beyond ACF and into a consideration of more critical and relational theories in sociology and geography, such as those developed by Doreen Massey, Bruno Latour, and Rosi Braidotti.

The spatiality and an ethics of dissent

So far, we have concentrated our attention on construing events of dissent as manifestations of coalitional advocacy associated with the re-articulation of a policy position, emerging from a systemic shock/rupture. Following the work of Sabatier (1986, 1988) and others associated with ACF, we have argued that an individual's engagement in an event of protest will be a reflection of their degree of cohesion to how the coalition frames the world of which they are a part (its ontology) and its ways of knowing about that world (the coalition as an epistemic community), but we must also consider a protestful act as occurring within a spatiality (whether that be material or digital). In Dorren Massey's book on the conceptual foundations of her critical relational geography, *For Space* (Massey, 2010), we are encouraged to recognise the importance of relationality to any construal of the spatial.

The space in which an event of dissent takes place is not an empty vessel that neutrally becomes the stage upon which the protest takes place. It is a significant actor within the event – as significant, and in many cases more significant, as that of the humans engaged in the protestful act. Whether that place is material, virtual, or hybrid, it becomes an active participant in what Massey refers to as the *event of place*. It is 'a constellation of processes rather than a thing. [It is] . . . open and internally multiple. Not capturable as a slice through time in the sense of an essential section. Not intrinsically coherent' (Massey, 2010, p. 141). Here, again, we can see multiplicity associated with conflictuality and contestation, opening up the spaces of dissent as ones of interest to CES. For those materially engaged in an act of protest, the protest occurs in a particular *here*,

> where spatial narratives meet up or form configurations, conjunctures of trajectories which have their own temporalities . . . an intertwining of histories in which the spatiality of those histories (their then as well as their here) is inescapably entangled.
>
> (Ibid, p. 139)

What Massey adds, which is significant, is the attribution of active participation of non-human actors within such a framework. The event of place imbues the spatiality of an event of dissent with an active participation in its manifestation – moving beyond it as the empty vessel in which the action takes place. In doing so, she consciously echoes the actor–network theory of Bruno Latour.

For Latour, actor–network theory (ANT) exceeds the limitations of the scope that was initially given by Callon and Law (1982) in their early discussion of how individual interest contributes to the binding together of groups (though even at that level, we can identify an association with ACF). He does this by problematising, while simultaneously accepting, each of its three terms (Latour, 2005).

Actors constitute and are constituted through their perspective and orientation as part of a network and not stable, fixed, nodes that act as foundational to the construction of that network. It is the web of their associations that are, to an extent, more significant than that towards which they are mono-directionally associated. Consequently, they reach beyond that which is human to include non-human materialities (plants, animals, resources, histories, environments, etc.) as well as institutions, discourses, and hegemonic frames of reference (though they will have material manifestations, such as the baton of the riot control officer or the carceral structures of a juridical system). Likewise, Latour problematises *network* for its connotations of stability and a presumption that information can pass through it without deformation. In Latour's ANT, networks evolve and adapt; they are fluid, they can burst into new multiplicities, and they can collapse into new nodes, with change and deformation taking place at every twist and turn. Such *networks* bear a closer resemblance to Deleuze and Guattari's construal of the rhizome – a point Latour was to make in an interview with Crawford (1997) when he said ' "Rhizome" is the perfect word for network. Actor–network theory should be called actant/rhizome ontology . . . because it is an ontology, it is about actants, and it is about rhizomes' (Latour & Crawford, 1993, p. 263).

This quotation also highlights Latour's problematisation of the use of 'theory' within ANT, arguing it needs to be approached as an ontology, as actants are constituted through their associations and not associations constituted through actants, rather than a theory that seeks to draw specific observations together. It is this spatiality of relationality/associativeness that leads us towards the ethics of protest, for it sets us on a path that can lead us from the notion of *being-with* in the work of Jean-Luc Nancy to the affirmative ethics of Rosi Braidotti.

Nancy, in *Being Singular Plural* argues that there is no *I* before the *We*, that all existence is co-existence. He writes, 'There is no meaning if meaning is not shared, and not because there would be an ultimate or first signification that all beings have in common, but because meaning is itself the sharing of Being' (Nancy, 2000, p. 2). It is such a relational sharing of being, and the limitations of that shared being, that becomes articulated through the collective action of dissent – a shared manifestation of human and non-human actants that 'constitutes a robust alternative to [a] state of anxiety' (Braidotti, 2023, p. 93) that affirms the actants and the manifestation (the act of protesting, the evental landscape of their dissent, and the public presentation of a counter-narrative expressing their coherence to a contesting coalitional narrative) of their ethical stance. Unlike utilitarianism, this does not provide us with a calculus for establishing if an action is *right* or *wrong*. Such a position does not obviate contestation and conflictuality around the ethical of narratives associated with dissent, because more than one *robust alternative* may be so constituted. It does, however, contribute to an ethical stance at the ontic and epistemic core of a coalition – a stance reflected in the individual participant's proximity to that which provides actants, within a coalition, with an affirmation of their ethical position.

Though this has been a rather whistlestop journey, covering points that a longer work would unpack in far greater detail, we have now reached a point of summation before moving into outlining our book's framework.

Summation

This book enquires into the mediated manifestation of protest events, both by public media platforms and the organisations engaged in events of dissent. It does this through the lens of critical event studies which, following Spracklen and Lamond (2016), focuses on the contested and conflictual narratives deployed to render communicable the multiplicity of possibilities emergent from what Sabatier and Weible (2007) refer to as a system shock.

System shocks produce coalitions, which could include social movements as well as media responses to protest, and legislative frameworks for the restriction of dissent. Coalitions form around alternative narratives associated with approaches to addressing the rupture that the shock(s) produces. Such coalitions have a core of ontic, epistemic, and, in the sense suggested by Braidotti (2023), an affirmative ethical stance. Depending on an individual's proximity to such core relationships, they may choose to engage in some form of direct action – seeking to realise their coalition's narrative for the resolution of the system shock. One form that action could take would be to participate in one or more events of dissent. Those at a remove from that core, as further information, or further aligned system shocks, may either migrate between different coalitions or move to a perspective that articulate neutral/no interest orientation in relation to the issue.

By investigating the mediated narratives associated with events of dissent, we can gain insight into how such events are articulated in the public realm, both by those engaged in protest action and those engaged in seeking to mitigate or obviate such action.

Chapter 1: The manifestation of events of dissent

In line with the conceptual framework for the book, in this chapter we will set out the significance of protest to CES. It will consider how critical event studies can be applied to events of dissent and the mediated articulation of the actions of social movements in the public realm (both material and virtual). As such, we ask – are events of dissent tools for innovation or simply the display of an angry mob? Through an examination of cross-cutting themes, discernible from the mediated framing of three case study protest interventions, we research the mediated evental landscape of protest and how it has been associated with socio-economic deprivation, affective spatialities of otherness, sociocultural shifts, and the narrative frames the mainstream press has applied to crowd behaviour. This highlights the distinction between peaceful protests and violent ones, as framed within their media portrayal and labelling.

Through a review of news media discourses attached to three movements for social justice, we examine contestation in the media reporting of the police and protesters' actions at targeted interventions instigated by Black Lives Matter, Reclaim These Streets (the Sarah Everard vigil of the 13th of March 2021), and Extinction Rebellion's blockade of News International's Broxbourne printworks on the 4th September 2020. We develop that into a reflection on the significance and meaning of space and place and the act of claim making mediated through media coverage and *public reaction.*

Chapter 2: Protests as individual experiences

Having considered the wider scale discourses associated with events of dissent and protest, this chapter interrogates the individual experience of protest participation. While, traditionally, events are understood in terms of their commercial and entertainment aspects (their spectacular dimensions), we suggest that activities and experiences surrounding social activism should also be acknowledged as part of the individual's lived experience of engaging with such events.

While we argue that the creative collaborations serve as meeting points for conversations between different worlds and social spheres (Shukaitis, 2009), we explore how individual characteristics affect an individual's experience of place (Massey, 2010) and also of being an activist. That discussion, in turn, raises questions about the lasting consequences of what the cognitive, relational, and emotional impacts can be on participants, when engaging in protest events (della Porta, 2008).

Through the investigation of the coverage and Internet backlash, associated with the Sarah Everard vigil, we look at a wider issue of public opinion forming based on the media's framing of the underlying issue – violence against women – as mediated attempts to manipulate. This leads to a further exploration of how aspects of the print-based news media have manipulated the notion and public understanding of democracy, regarding the coverage of Extinction Rebellion's blockade of News International's Broxbourne printworks.

Chapter 3: Organising events of dissent

In this chapter, we delve deeper into how events of dissent facilitate network building, strengthen the sense of social identity, reinforce the meaning of shared purpose, and contribute to social and cultural capital of those engaged in events of dissent. We analyse Black Lives Matter, Extinction Rebellion, and Reclaim These Streets' use of digital technologies. Not only do we consider the role such platforms can have in organising and promoting protest events, and the building of activist networks, but we also discuss a darker side of the Internet, one that highlights the conflictual realities of digital communications. As well as reflecting on how digital participation can create new sites of engagement (Jones, 2005) and forge new norms of interaction and identity, we recognise how it also provides those standing in opposition to those protesting with a route into articulating more sinister counter narratives. Although the Internet is often perceived as democratising – providing an accessible and inclusive public sphere, it also facilitates new ways to articulate ridicule, hatred, and exclusion.

Chapter 4: Articulating events of dissent

In this chapter, we continue the exploration into the power structures behind the media narratives and the use of those narratives for identity construction, and we analyse the power geometries in physical and virtual spaces as sites of engagement.

Herman and Chomsky's propaganda model is then used to evaluate the protest event coverage in a sample of right, left, and centre-leaning newspapers. Political opportunity theory proposed by Edwards (2014) is supported by the comparison of the media's framing of the police actions at the selected sample of protest events. We look into how the reporters' ideological lens can result in misinformation, emission, and carving events into the narratives of binary *us* versus *them*. This is followed by the analysis of selective exposure, online trending, audience segmentation, and bias creation through algorithms and bots, which are relatively new concerns associated specifically with online media sources; however, they become more perturbing as the consumption of news online grows and the audiences remain unaware or unable to control the choices or sources of the information that reaches them.

Chapter 5: The eventalisation of the political

In this final chapter, we will begin by drawing together the strands of the various arguments developed through the preceding chapters. This discussion frames key aspect of that debate as an example of the manifestation of contemporary political engagement, in late capitalist/neo-liberal democracies as an eventalisation of the political, forming what Lamond and Reid (2017) have referred to as a *democracy of the spectacle*. The chapter will close through a reiteration of the role of power and associated struggles around contested narratives we argued as the core of understanding the mediated manifestation of events of dissent. We will align that discussion with current policy and media debates around the management of events of dissent – drawing on recent protest, including current industrial action, with recent UK legislation around restricting the right to protest and the forms that protest can take.

Chapter 6: Final remarks – in conversation with ...

The book encompasses media analysis associated with the framing and manipulation of the imaginary of protest, as well as drawing on the lived experience of some people whose lives have been substantially affected by their engagement with dissent as activists. In our final chapter, we revisit two of those people, giving them the opportunity to articulate the final comments of the book. In conversation, we ask them to reflect on some of the book's broader themes; how their activism has impacted them and their well-being, and how they view the association between events of dissent and the media. Our research barely scratches the surface of the research that needs to be done on protest and social movements within a CES frame of reference, but it opens up several possible trajectories within the field. Those trajectories are conceptual and empirical, they are highly abstract and visceral. It seemed most fitting to close our book with voices articulating the lived experience of some of those working for change, within advocacy coalitions.

Note

1 Emphasis my own; however, the italicisation in the text matches the words in the original, which form hyperlinks to other definitions within the Collins Dictionary website.

References

Braidotti, R. (2023) Affirmative ethics, new materialism and the posthuman convergence. In Capua, G. & Oosterbeek, L. (Eds.) *Bridges to global ethics: Geoethics at the confluence of humanities and sciences*, pp. 93–108. Springer.

Bringel, B. M., & Domingues, J. M. (Eds.). (2015) *Global modernity and social contestation*. Sage.

Callon, M., & Law, J. (1982) On interests and their transformation: Enrolment and counter-enrolment. *Social Studies of Science* 12(4), 615–625.

Colinsdictionary.com (2022) Definition of 'permacrisis'. www.collinsdictionary.com/dictionary/english/permacrisis Last accessed: 21/07/2023.

della Porta, D. (2008) Eventful protest, global conflicts. *Distinktion: Journal of Social Theory* 9(2), 27–56.

Diani, M., & Mische, A. (2015) Network approaches and social movements. In Della Porta, D. & Diani, M. (Eds.) *The Oxford handbook of social movements*. Oxford University Press.

Duric, L., Kennell, J., Vujicic, M. D., Stamenkovic, I., & Farkic, J. (2022) Protest events as institutions: Stakeholders perceptions of the changing role of Serbia's EXIT festival. *International Journal of Event and Festival Management*. DOI: 10.1108/IJEFM-04-2022-0023.

Edwards, G. (2014) *Social movements and protests – key topics in sociology*. Cambridge University Press.

Feigenbaum A., Frenzel F., & McCurdy P. (2013) *Protest Camps: Imagining Alternative Worlds*. London: Zed Books.

Gerbaudo, P. (2012) *Tweets and the streets: Social media and contemporary activism*. Pluto Press.

Getz, D., & Page, S. J. (2020) *Event studies: Theory, research, and policy for planned events*. 4th ed. Routledge.

Gubernat, R., & Rammelt, H. (2017) Recreative activism in Romania: How cultural affiliation and lifestyle yield political engagement. *Socio. Hu társadalomtudományi szemle: Social Science Review* 5, 143–163. DOI: 10.18030/socio.hu.2017en.143

Home Office (2023) *Official statistics: Hate crime, England, and Wales, 2022 to 2023*. 2nd ed. www.gov.uk/government/statistics/hate-crime-england-and-wales-2022-to-2023/hate-crime-england-and-wales-2022-to-2023 Last accessed: 03/11/2023.

Howard-Grenville, J., Golden-Biddle, K., Irwin, J., & Mao, J. (2011) Liminality as cultural process for cultural change. *Organization Science* 22(2), 522–539.

Jenkins-Smith, H., Silva, C. L., Gupta, K., & Ripberger, J. T. (2014) Belief system continuity and change in policy advocacy coalitions: Using cultural theory to specify belief systems, coalitions, and sources of change. *Policy Studies Journal* 42(4), 484–508.

Jones, F. (2019) *Reclaiming our space: How Black Feminists are changing the world from the tweets to the streets*. Beacon Press.

Jones, R. H. (2005) Sites of engagement as sites of attention: Time, space, and culture in electronic discourse. In Norris, S. & Jones, R. H. (Eds.) *Discourse in action: Introducing mediated discourse analysis*. Routledge, pp. 141–154.

Lamond, I. R. (2019) Conceptualising events of dissent: Understanding the Lava Jato rally in Sao Paulo, 5 December 2017. In Finkel, R., Sharp, B. & Sweeny, M. (Eds.) *Accessibility, inclusion, and diversity in critical event studies*. Routledge, pp. 150–164.

Lamond, I. R., & Reid, C. (2017) *The 2015 UK general election and the 2016 EU Referendum: Towards a democracy of the spectacle*. Palgrave Macmillan.

Latour, B. (2005) *Reassembling the social: An introduction to actor-network theory*. Oxford University Press.

Latour, B., & Crawford, T. H. (1993) An interview with Bruno Latour. *Configurations* 1(2), 247–268.

Massey, D. (2010) *For space*. Sage.

Matti, S., & Sandstrom, A. (2013) The defining elements of advocacy coalitions: Continuing the search for explanations for coordination and coalition structures. *Review of Policy Research* 30(2), 240–257.

Meijerink, S. (2005) Understanding policy stability and change. The interplay of advocacy coalitions and epistemic communities, windows of opportunity, and Dutch coastal flooding policy 1945–2003. *Journal of European Public Policy* 12(6), 1060–1077.

Nancy, J. (2000) *Being singular plural*. Trans. Richardson, R. D. & O'Byrne, A. E. Stanford University Press.

ONS (2023) LABD: Labour disputes in the UK. www.ons.gov.uk/employmentandlabourmarket/peopleinwork/workplacedisputesandworkingconditions/datasets/labdlabourdisputesintheuk Last accessed: 21/07/2023.

Pernecky, T. (2016) *Approaches and methods in event studies*. Routledge.

Pielichaty, H. (2015) Festival space: Gender, liminality and the carnivalesque. *International Journal of Event and Festival Management* 6(3), 235–250.

Rodríguez-Campo, L., Braña-Rey, F., Alén-González, E., & Fraiz-Brea, J. A. (2021) The liminality in popular festivals: Identity, belonging and hedonism as values of tourist satisfaction. In *Liminality in tourism*. Routledge, pp. 11–31.

Rovisco, M., & Ong, J. C. (Eds.). (2016) *Taking the square: Mediated dissent and the occupation of public space*. Rowman & Littlefield.

Sabatier, P. A. (1986) Top-down and bottom-up approaches to implementation research: A critical analysis and suggested synthesis. *Journal of Public Policy* 6(1), 21–48.

Sabatier, P. A. (1988) An advocacy coalition framework of policy change and the role of policy-oriented learning therein. *Policy Sciences* 21(2–3), 129–168.

Sabatier, P. A., & Weible, C. M. (2007) The advocacy coalition framework. In Sabatier, P. A. & Weible, C. M. (Eds.) *Theories of the policy process*. 2nd ed. Routledge.

Shukaitis, S. (2009) *Imaginal machines: Autonomy & self-organization in the revolutions of everyday life*. Autonomedia.

Smith, A. (2015) *Events in the city: Using public space as event venues*. Routledge.

Söderlund, J., & Borg, E. (2018) Liminality in management and organization studies: Process, position, and place. *International Journal of Management Reviews* 20(4), 880–902.

Spracklen, K., & Lamond, I. R. (2016) *Critical event studies.* Routledge.

Touraine, A. (2000) *Can we live together: Equality and difference.* Trans. Macey, D. Polity Press.

Turner, V. W. (2017 [1969]) *The ritual process: Structure and anti-structure.* Routledge.

Wagner-Pacifici, R. (2017) *What is an event?* Chicago University Press.

Weible, C. M., Sabatier, P. A., Jenkins-Smith, H. C., Nohrstedt, D., Henry, A. D., & DeLeon, P. (2011) A quarter century of the advocacy coalition framework: An introduction to the special issue. *Policy Studies Journal* 39(3), 349–360.

Wittgenstein, L. (2009 [1953]) *Philosophical investigations.* Trans. Anscombe, G. E. M., Hacker, P. M. S. & Schulte, J. Wiley-Blackwell.

Zadeh, L. A. (1965) Fuzzy sets. *Information and Control* 8(3), 338–353.

1 The manifestation of events of dissent

1.1 Events of dissent and event studies

Although protests are far from being a new phenomenon, very few event management writers discuss events of social activism in their event typology, which poses a question of how events are viewed and understood by the industry and academia, whether they are only regarded from the commercial point of view or seen as sociocultural constructs, and whether the disciplinary constraints impose limits on the interdisciplinary approaches (Getz & Ziakas, 2020). The academic world may appear impartial, but it is critical to remember that the advancement of certain fields and research can be influenced by the state and dominant powers, and scholars might offer certain trades, industries, or political parties less direct (or less visible) forms of intellectual support and advocacy (Murphy, 2020). As stated by Edward Bernays, 'the state university prospers according to the extent to which it can sell itself to the people of the state' (Bernays, 2004, p. 138). Willingly or unwillingly, the academics may become caught in the power play of political and economic forces in a situation that echoes Herman and Chomsky's propaganda model (Herman & Chomsky, 1988). The impact of such power play can manifest in the availability or lack of research works on certain topics, the views and arguments conveyed and backed by the academics or discipline, as well as the opportunities and openings for future research.

Traditionally, events are discussed in terms of their commercial and entertainment characteristics; however, Lamond and Spracklen (2015) assert it is time to acknowledge the fact that even radical political movements and activism are closely related and form part of the event management subject field, and many activities and spaces surrounding social activism can be seen as events – 'protests are events, and events are sites of protest' (Lamond & Spracklen, 2015, p. 3). Since the beginning of the 20th century, protests have come a long way evolving from the workers' strikes to music and showmanship events and media and art spectacles. Cable (2015a) outlines the ideas of various scholars who analyse social movements and protests and quotes Lipsky's (1968, cited in Cable 2015a, p. 60) definition of protest activity 'as a mode of political action oriented toward objection to one or more policies or

DOI: 10.4324/9781003460640-2

conditions, characterized by showmanship or display of an unconventional nature'. Throughout history, contentious events and protests played a significant role in the evolution and transformation of social, cultural, and political processes, enabling the development of collective experiences and interactions between different social actors, creating 'concentrated transformations . . . in those highly visible events that end up symbolizing entire social movements' (della Porta, 2008, p. 30).

1.2   Protests as instruments of change

The concepts of innovation and change are central to the history and development of humankind, as social, cultural, and political innovations drive the creation and formation of our societies and politics. Mars (2013a) states that a process innovation requires a novel approach which brings significant gains in society and the human condition, and innovative products and processes often work in tandem to create advancement as one can enable the other. Usually, the grounds for innovation are the demands to find a solution to pressing problems, discover strategies to achieve desired change and seek out ways to address unmet needs, and ongoing issues in the marketplace or society, and the result of innovation must both lead to some level of 'creative destruction' in the field and have a lasting positive impact (Mars, 2013b). If innovation aims to solve a pressing issue, then in terms of political, environmental, and cultural innovations, a protest can be seen as a tool that helps to drive the desired change. White (2016) agrees that protests are one of many instruments for devising social change, and dissent is necessary for social growth and renewal.

Visibility and novelty of a protest are important attributes that captivate attention and impact the public consciousness, and it is here that the innovations in other fields, such as technology, aid the purpose of the event and work in collaboration with the novel strategies implemented as part of the event itself. Lefebvre (2004, p. 14) believes that for a change to the repeating and familiar life rhythms within a society or culture to eventually occur, a group of people who designate themselves as innovators must first 'intervene by imprinting a rhythm on an era', and their 'acts must inscribe themselves on reality'. Creative alliances that serve as meeting points for conversations between different worlds and social spheres are often places where social movements form (Shukaitis, 2009b), and where those movements can welcome the public and the media into the conversation. Della Porta (2008, p. 48) suggests that protests can be considered particularly 'eventful' when they have 'a highly relevant cognitive, relational and emotional impact on participants and beyond participants', especially when the chains of events or cycles of protests, inclusive communication, and free spaces to allow for the relational mechanisms and identity to develop are present. Employing protests as acts of disruption or declarations of disapproval is a distinctive feature of social movements and one that the public at large tend to associate with the social movements because protests are the 'visible signs that tell us that a collective effort at social change is underway' (Edwards, 2014, p. 6). The innovative or disruptive nature of a protest will draw the public's attention; however, journalist and radio producer Zoë Blackler (Knapp, 2022) also argues that the need for a more disruptive event can be initiated by the media itself – the journalists may be keen to explore the cause or the issue the protesters are bringing to the public's attention; however, due to the news outlet's political leaning or vested interests, they may not be able to do so, and therefore protest event coverage may be the only avenue for this conversation to be had; so ever more arresting or more obstreperous event becomes a prerequisite. We will explore this in more detail in Chapter 4.

1.2.1   *Dissent and human emotion*

Explorative research of protest as a relatively new type of event requires the researcher to allow for flexibility in their inquiry into the subtle and often indistinct human experiences. As protest and social movements remain a sensitive and often contentious subject, it is important to look into the roots of the proposed binary of 'good' versus 'evil' which is often seen in the news and sometimes implied in research. Propaganda and persuasion techniques used in public relations are known to make use of emotional triggers instead of rational arguments to solicit the desired response, often without much concern for potential underlying ethical issues (Fawkes, 2007). In his exploration of early history of propaganda, Chomsky (1991) claims that the first modern government propaganda operation took place in the middle of the World War I. As the war raged in Europe, US population saw no reason to become involved in this war, but the newly elected president Woodrow Wilson had different views and so he established a government propaganda commission (Creel Commission) which, within six months, successfully turned pacifistic citizens into 'a hysterical, war-mongering population which wanted to destroy everything German, tear the German limb from limb, go to war and save the world'. The next step following this successful campaign and the end of the war was to 'whip up a hysterical Red Scare' which, with strong support from the media – the business establishment which organised and carried out much of this work – culminated in 'eliminating such dangerous problems as freedom of the press and freedom of political thought'. The means of propaganda used in those campaigns were extensive, a lot of it was invented by the British propaganda, and there was no reluctance to fabricate the atrocities committed by the enemy in order 'to direct the thought of most of the world' (Chomsky, 1991).

Popular media sources and even some academics tend to frame protests by using traditional 'angry mob' and 'mob mentality' concepts, which originate in historic 'crowd psychology' popularised by Gustave le Bon and Herbert Blumer (Edwards, 2014, p. 21). Castells (2015, p. 246) believes that it is anger about the existing conditions that would suppress any fear of being involved in risky protest activities, as he states that social movements are triggered by emotion and a crisis in living conditions 'that make life unbearable for most people'. It is unsurprising, then, that in the public's mind, there is a link between the protests against the established system and the images of angry crowds driven by raw emotion. Nevertheless, a protest can take many different forms. Often, the success of a protest lies in the ability of the organisers and participants to find the ways to 'scramble the expectations and normal flow of social life, and thus at least for a second open a possibility for some other form of communication and interaction to occur' (Shukaitis, 2009a, p. 72). Sometimes, after the disappearance of certain forms of collectivism from the political realm, it may return in other, more artistic and creative forms, through the use of new imagery and symbols, such as the science fiction films, new art forms, and expressions (Shukaitis, 2009a) that enable the criticism of what doesn't work in the society to be expressed without openly criticising it but by exaggerating its absurdity (Shukaitis, 2009b, p. 102). Although in public mind, a mention of protests will often summon images of angry crowds, a lot of historic protests took peaceful and creative forms, uniting people and enabling for the sentiment to be shared through songs (The Singing Revolution), performances (Duran Adam's Standing Man), and claiming space (Baltic Way, also known as Chain of Freedom). In April 2023, Extinction Rebellion organised 'The Big One', an event which attracted approximately 100,000 participants and was run in cooperation with the police. Nonetheless, shared images and understandings may not always have the same meaning to those within the movement or event and the passers-by. As Shukaitis (2009a, p. 76) points out, when protesters chant 'this is what democracy looks like', the bystanders may wonder 'if a street demonstration is really an embodiment of democracy', overlooking the fact that the chants refer to the process of horizontal organisation and participation that lead to the action.

1.2.2 What makes events of dissent

Protest events as tools for innovation and change marked many a turning point in human history and society. To help differentiate protests from other events, Edwards (2014) suggests four conceptual distinctions that form the understanding of what a social movement is. Aside from employing protests as instruments in pursuit of change, social movements are formed of collective and organised action and they are usually durable movements that exist for some time, while members of social movements not only work and interact together, they also share a collective identity and understanding of the purpose – a sense of 'we'– reinforced by shared beliefs and solidarity (Edwards, 2014; della Porta, 2008). The shared identity and purpose offer a counter-frame to the legitimised framing of the existing regime and call for meaningful work in creating the change through collective action (della Porta et al., 2006).

Despite the underlying assumption that the catalyst for a protest or a social movement is a grievance or social deprivation, researchers have not been able to find strong correlations between socio-economic deprivation and 'disturbances' (Edwards, 2014, p. 16). Instead, involvement in the social movements and participation in protests have been attributed to emotional values and cultural shifts (Blumer, quoted in Edwards, 2014, p. 17) and the narratives and interpretations of the societal problems – the 'frames' that the activists form to help the wider public understand the change needed (Edwards, 2014; della Porta et al., 2006).

1.3   Framing of events of dissent during the COVID-19 pandemic

It is easy to discern that the media and state powers tend to frame protests as something disruptive, and in this book we briefly explore three events that took place during the COVID-19 pandemic – the Black Lives Matter UK protests that followed George Floyd's murder in the United States on 25th May 2020, Extinction Rebellion blockade of Ruper Murdoch's printworks at Broxbourne on the night of 4th September 2020, and Sarah Everard vigil organised by Reclaim These Streets on 13th March 2021 – to demonstrate how the established media frames and public attitudes diverge, change, and expand depending on the cause of the event. The worldwide pandemic and restrictions that were in place created a truly unique emotional, legal, and cognitive setting for the Black Lives Matter, Extinction Rebellion, and Reclaim These Streets events. As many aspects of people's ordinary lives were halted, there were more time and focus to consider what was legal and lawful and right or wrong and to really notice how the government and institutions exercised their powers over individuals.

To evaluate Herman and Chomsky's propaganda model, we compared the coverage of those three events in a small sample of left-wing, right-wing, and centre-leaning newspapers. We focused on the news coverage and opinion pieces published over five days surrounding the protests (two days before the event, the day of the event, and two days following the event) to reflect the most instant reactions and coverage. *The Guardian* was selected as the left-leaning, and *The Telegraph* was chosen as the right-leaning newspaper, and we used online archives to obtain the historic issues of both papers. Chosen movements and events differed in their purpose, thus allowing for an independent analysis of data with no obvious connections present among the supporters and media coverage of the movements. At the time, it seemed that the government, the police, and the media in the UK deliberated what was the right thing to do; however, as we will see, the approach to and the narratives surrounding the protests changed with the cause of the movement. The principal theme connecting the coverage of the three events in question is that the distinction between peaceful protests and violent ones may not always be evident but rather be partially determined by how the media portray and label them (Trottier & Fuchs, 2015, p. 32). The inconsistencies in the approach taken by the same media sources when reporting on the police actions, the safety measures, and the protesters' behaviours at separate events highlight the shifting agenda and interests reaching beyond the articles. Borrowing from Milliband, Trottier and Fuchs (2015, p. 29) suggest that the purpose of the informational aspect of mass media is to communicate the meaning of the existing regime to the citizens while reinforcing the existing social order. In current times, when information overload via numerous sources and means is ever present, the real value is arguably not the information but the amount of attention it can attract, and how this attention can be promoted and reproduced in service of particular ideologies (Jones, 2005). Those ideas and following analysis also support the political opportunity structure theory (Edwards, 2014) which suggests that political opportunity existing in the context surrounding protest events can be fairly open and welcoming to some movements or issues but closed to others. We will begin by examining the newspaper coverage of the events in question and delve into deeper exploration of the purpose, significance, and future of protests and their relationship with the power of the state in the following chapters of the book.

1.3.1   Black Lives Matter – May–June 2020

It is interesting to observe that despite the COVID-19-related restrictions imposed on public gatherings and social distancing, the first few protests associated with the Black Lives Matter movement that were held in the UK as part of the global wave of outcry at George Floyd's death received little-to-no coverage by the media. The only mention of early London protests is found in the words of eulogy delivered at George Floyd's memorial service as McGreal (2020) reported to *The Guardian* from Minneapolis on the 5th June. On the 1st of June 2020 reporting from the United States for *The Daily Telegraph*, Riley-Smith and Sabur's (2020) article analysed the situation in the United States but only contained one sentence to acknowledge that 'in London yesterday thousands marched in protest at police violence, chanting "no justice, no peace" '. The absence of reporting on what seemed to be a large-scale event involving 'thousands' posed the question for reasoning as to why the events received no press coverage. There is room for speculation. Was the absence of disruption and violence the reason for the lack of press attention, or were the protests deemed not important because they were held in response and support of something happening overseas? Perhaps the newspapers were yet undecided which side they should take on such a sensitive subject. So, we looked at the media coverage of protests that took place on the 6th and 7th June 2020 instead.

The Telegraph *and the* Daily Mail

Surprisingly, only a few articles could be found in *The Telegraph*, and there-fore one more right-leaning tabloid (the *Daily Mail*) was added to the newspa-per sample. On the 7th June, Sawer and Lowe (2020) reported that 'thousands of people went down on one knee' in London while 'similar expressions of solidarity' took place in other UK cities 'to voice anger at the death of Mr Floyd, as well as wider racist violence and discrimination', and after a day of 'overwhelmingly peaceful protests across the country, a section of the London march descended into ugly violence', resulting in a police officer fall-ing from her horse and being taken to hospital. The article quoted a Conserva-tive MP saying: 'it wasn't surprising the horse bolted when spooked by the flares and missiles and bikes being thrown'. While Home Secretary Priti Patel condemned the violence stating that 'protests must be peaceful and in accord-ance with social distancing rules' (Sawer & Lowe, 2020), the article pointed out that during the clashes, several people chanted for peace and 'told others to stop throwing objects'. The Mayor of London Sadiq Khan was not only quoted praising peaceful protesters but also said those who became violent 'let down the cause'. There was a mention of celebrities joining the marches, and activists were quoted explaining that the killing of George Floyd 'struck a match with everyone. Not just black people'.

The following day, Evans (2020) reported on 'a second night of violence' in London, while a police officer from Bristol said: 'we made a very tactical deci-sion that to stop people from doing that [toppling a statue of the slave trader] may have caused further disorder'. The Prime Minister Boris Johnson was said to have tweeted about people having a right to protest peacefully while observ-ing social distancing. Reporting on the estimated 10,000 people ignoring the health warnings at the gathering in Bristol, event that resulted in the statue of a slave trader Edward Colston being brought down, Evans pointed out that many of those involved were white, briefly drawing attention to the incident that took place in London when a police officer's horse 'bolted and careered into traffic lights' and claiming that 'almost 30 police officers have been injured in the violence in recent days' as Mayor of London condemned the violence. Camber, Groves, and Brown of the *Daily Mail* (2020) made an interesting comparison: 'in echoes of the fall of Saddam Hussein, a masked mob tore down a statue of 17th century slave trader Edward Colston in Bristol'. One police officer was reported to be recovering in hospital, and the Home Secretary was quoted feel-ing 'sickened' by George Floyd's death and insisting that 'justice and account-ability must follow', although unlawful behaviour and disorder caused by 'a small minority of violent people using the guise of peaceful protest to pursue reckless lawlessness' in the UK and 'the utterly appalling abuse of our police officers' could not be excused. The article claimed there had been 'privately . . . disquiet among some senior ministers about the softly-softly approach adopted by police when the demonstrations began to get ugly'. The article also quoted a police superintendent saying that the force had decided to take a 'neighbourhood policing approach' to the protest to avoid causing tensions, as the organisers of Black Lives Matter were reported to distance themselves and claim that the statue had 'nothing to do' with them.

The Guardian

On the 7th June, Tim Adams (2020) wrote for *The Guardian* describing the 'coming together of mostly young people in our cities under the Black Lives Matter' as an expression of 'emotional catharsis' after the months of lock-down, as 'many thousands crammed shoulder to shoulder' in London ignoring the police and government warnings about the risk of virus transmission. The protest 'felt very much like the beginning of something . . . a sustainable expression of the need for change' as 'innumerable wounds have been opened . . . stretching back in British memories over generations – the protesters' banners were a roll call of past and current injustice', said Adams (2020), enforcing the notion that the protesters gathered not only to show solidarity with what was happening in America but rather to address the injustices that still exist on the local soil. Those intentions were expressed in the actor John Boyega's speech: 'We are a physical representation of our support for George Floyd. . . . We are a physical representation of our support for Stephen Lawrence'. 'The loose network of Black Lives Matter activists' coordinated the protests across the UK, wrote Adams (2020), and 'did their best to mitigate the risks in the crowd . . . equipped . . . with stocks of free masks and sanitiser'. One of the organisers, Imarn Ayton, was quoted saying that she didn't want to see any alcohol or weed as it was 'not a carnival', and people needed to keep their distance as 'coronavirus is killing black people'. Ayton said:

> [I]t feels like a different moment . . . the death of George Floyd the protest has inspired many more people to speak up, black, white, everyone. . . . People are no longer prepared to be ignorant; they want to educate themselves.
>
> (Adams, 2020)

Out of several activists that were given voice in the article, one claimed they felt they had no real choice but to be there and regretted that it had taken a death of a person to gather people together. Another activist highlighted the high numbers of COVID deaths in the black communities and black people suffering economically. A participant who held a sign that said 'Your silence is violence' summed up:

> [I]f you are young and you are not speaking up now, then it definitely says who you are. They don't have to be here physically because we are in the middle of a pandemic, but if they are not here mentally and in spirit, well f***'em.
>
> (Adams, 2020)

The demonstrators and activists had not only 'been motivated by more than revulsion [to the video of the violent murder of George Floyd]' but also by 'acknowledging a fundamental truth' of understanding the killing as a symptom of systemic racism, and 'by building their campaign around that reality they have promoted radical and challenging conversations . . . about the nature of racism and the actions that people of all races can take in eliminating it', wrote historian and broadcaster David Olusoga (2020) in *The Guardian*. He reported that young people of all ethnicities had been inspired by the Black Lives Matter, and the protests had morphed into a worldwide anti-racist movement which 'both online and on the streets' was 'calling out racism wherever it exists and in whatever forms it is found'. And still, Olusoga (2020) writes,

> [A]lmost instantly a predictable chorus of voices, emanating from predictable corners of British public life, rose up to dismiss the whole thing as an irrelevance. Using a familiar playbook, they accused those black Britons . . . of making false comparisons [with the US],

as he listed the statistics of black people being stop searched, arrested, and imprisoned in the UK, claiming the 'bad habit' of 'excusing or downplaying British racism' continued its long history, which he outlined in the article.

1.3.2   *Extinction Rebellion – blockade of Broxbourne printworks – September 2020*

Rupert Murdoch's Broxbourne printworks' blockade was chosen for this analysis as it offered a perfect opportunity to observe how the media sources reacted to an event that impacted printed media distribution. The event took place on the night of the 4th September 2020 and continued into the following morning, as a group of XR members blocked the roads leading to the Broxbourne printworks intending to 'expose the failure of those publications to accurately report on the climate and ecological emergency, their divisive tactics, the consistent manipulation of the truth by their corporate owners to suit their own personal and political agendas' (Extinction Rebellion, 2021).

The Daily Telegraph *and* The Sunday Telegraph

The coverage of the event by *The Daily Telegraph* and *The Sunday Telegraph* focused on three main themes: police inaction, XR attempt to prevent free speech, and XR criminal activities. Bird and Malnick (2020) condemned the police 'for failing to halt a demonstration intended to stifle the freedom of the press' as Hertfordshire Constabulary's chief constable was quoted saying that his force was 'committed to facilitation of peaceful protest and ensuring compliance . . . instead of dispersing the crowd'. The same article quoted the former head of the Metropolitan's counter-terrorism command who said the activist group 'had shifted from mere protesters into organising planned criminality and should be treated as such', and a Labour MP who called for the police to 'uphold the law, enable people to go to work and read the papers they choose'. Bird and Malnick (2020) questioned why no activists or organisers had been fined on the night of the event 'for breaching the rules meant to prevent gatherings of 30 or more people during coronavirus restrictions'. The reporters appeared confused that 'despite claiming to be climate change protesters, many activists said they were against the perceived political stance of some newspapers'. According to the article, the XR statement said the action was about racism, as well 'immigration policy, the rights and treatment of minority groups' and other issues, and Bird and Malnick (2020) claimed that 'this shift' was seen by 'many' as making XR a political movement rather than a campaign group. Interestingly, we will see that this framing never appeared in the coverage of the Reclaim These Streets vigil although the movement was aimed at challenging the systemic treatment of women by the police and the patriarchy in general.

In *The Sunday Telegraph*, Tominey (2020) claimed that it was already known that 'The so-called 'progressive Left' believes the silencing of dissenting views is a legitimate campaign tactic. Feted by the liberal establishment . . . this cabal of eco-fascists has always believed its right to trump ours'. Same article stated that by barricading the UK's three largest printing presses, 'XR has finally shown how anti-democratic it actually is'. Tominey described XR activists as 'deluded crusties' and 'civil disobedients' and claimed the fact that the police 'felt the need to double down on its support of "the right to peaceful protest" . . . tells you . . . why XR keeps getting away with holding this country to ransom'. She mused whether we were in a parallel universe where COVID-19 rules could be flouted by claiming to be 'saving the planet'. In a rather revealing and self-contradictory statement, Tominey wrote 'As with Black Lives Matter, hard left zealots joining XR are more concerned with bringing down capitalism than honouring the founding principles'. She then found relief in her conviction that 'the silent majority understands you can never win an argument for free speech by suppressing the free speech of others' and ended with a statement 'the truth has been freed, the Extinction Rebellion has been found out'. Malnick (2020) quoted his 'Whitehall sources' saying the XR was 'not your normal protest group' and needed to be looked at 'in a different way', introducing the news of ministers considering new powers, making it easier for the police to crack down on protests 'and explicitly outlawing disruption to tenets of democracy'. The article claimed discussions had taken place whether XR 'could even be proscribed as a terror organisation, but the source said it was thought to be highly unlikely that it would meet the legal threshold for such move', despite the Policy Exchange report in 2019 claiming 'XR should be treated as an extremist anarchist group after finding it had a "subversive" agenda rooted in the "political extremism of anarchism" rather than just campaigning on climate change'. An XR spokesman was reported to have claimed that such agenda was the one 'espoused by the Government'.

In *The Daily Telegraph*, Conservative MP and Secretary of State for Digital, Culture, Media and Sport, Oliver Dowden (2020) condemned XR for the 'ugly irony of silencing newspapers', claiming that newspapers 'including The Telegraph have dedicated a huge amount of coverage' to climate change. He deemed it ironic that by blocking the presses, XR 'deprived Sun readers of an interview with Sir David Attenborough, silencing the most passionate of campaigners', but 'for the modern Left, facts take second place to virtue signalling and platform denying'. Dowden (2020) declared that the Prime Minister had already said that 'climate change is an issue critical to the future of our country', posing that as a counter-argument to the activists' 'strongly held beliefs' and shaming the 'stupid minority of eco anarchists' for attempting to 'censor' the media which had already 'battled through the disruption of the coronavirus and the threat of long-term media consumer trends' and for leaving 'countless people . . . including elderly and potentially vulnerable readers' without their morning papers which they 'rely on . . . to stay connected and engaged'. Taking it even further, *The Daily Telegraph*'s Mendick, Gatten and Swerling (2020) paraphrased XR activist and *The Independent* columnist Donnachadh Mccarthy to title their article 'Newspapers are like Nazis, says organiser of blockade'. The article included the actual quotes that read:

> [T]his is like World War Two and you guys [the newspapers] are on the other side. . . . It puts you on the side of the existential threat. It is a different existential threat, but it is a bigger one than the Nazis.

The paraphrasing had two obvious inaccuracies. First, Mccarthy referred to the 'existential threat' not the newspapers. Second, the omission of the actual words that were spoken allowed Mendic, Gatten, and Swerling to suggest that Mccarthy used 'you guys' to address the newspapers in general; however, given the fact that McCarthy himself writes opinion pieces for *The Independent* it would be safe to assume that he would not have meant all the newspapers or the media in general. The article continued speculating that the 'use of Second World War analogy will cause upset because of the association of the Nazis with burning books and shutting down of newspapers' and suggesting that according to the 'insiders', XR had struggled to make headlines as COVID-19 'put climate change on the back-burner', claiming there had been 'battles over accusations that the movement was too white and middle class . . . that the movement had failed to address racism in the police'. Perhaps revealingly, the same article interviewed a former XR activist who confirmed that future actions against media were likely and questioned whether the 'more overtly left-wing organisation' would continue with their previous strategy to bring journalists from the right-wing media onside. In a different article, Gatten (2020) pressed the idea that XR was losing activists and supporters, quoting an anonymous ex-activist saying that XR 'divisive and partisan culture war tactics' didn't make sense as the journalists from the papers affected by the blockade 'have been working hard to report the climate crisis while thousands of people from every part of the UK are tackling it'. Gatten (2020) then mentioned a statement made by XR in 2019 that said 'This is not a calling out of all media, but a calling in of those that work at the Daily Mail, Mail Online, Mail on Sunday, Daily Telegraph and The Sun'.

The Guardian

Addressing the blockade, *The Guardian*'s Iqbal (2020) informed that the presses affected by it were owned by Rupert Murdoch's News Corp and were used to print *The Sun, Times, Sun on Sunday, Sunday Times, The Daily Telegraph, The Sunday Telegraph*, the *Daily Mail, Mail on Sunday*, and the *London Evening Standard*. The article presented both sides of the argument as it quoted the Prime Minister say:

> [A] free press is vital in holding the government and other powerful institutions to account on issues . . . including the fight against climate change . . . [and] it is completely unacceptable to seek to limit the public's access to news in this way.

The article not only cited other political reactions but also published the XR statement on the matter which said:

> Our free press, society and democracy is under attack – from a failing government that lies to us constantly. . . . . Our leaders have allowed the majority of our media to be amassed in the hands of five people with powerful vested interests and deep connection to fossil fuel industries. We need a free press but we do not have it.
>
> (Iqbal, 2020)

Iqbal (2020) interviewed Steve Tooze, a former tabloid journalist who claimed to have worked for every of the affected newspapers in the past, and who joined the press blockade to support 'one day with far less misinformation, division and hate', stating that as a former insider, he also held blame for omitting important information and 'not telling the public what is really happening', which allows the government to avoid the pressures of the public on the important matters that the public had not been made aware of. The article relayed criticism from the Society of Editors, Guardian Media Group, and David Attenborough, who had largely supported XR in the past but admitted that their actions 'was not sensible politics' (Iqbal, 2020). The article by Slawson and Waterson (2020) not only identified the owners of the newspapers impacted by the print press blockade but also highlighted the fact that the printing had been transferred to other 'industry partners' overnight to enable the delivery of the newspapers to retailers. A spokesperson for Newsprinters was quoted apologising to all the readers who were unable to buy their papers due to late deliveries and claimed that XR actions were an 'attack on all of the free press' and had impacted 'many workers going about their jobs', calling for action from the police and the Home Office. The article clarified that a small number of Guardian home-delivery subscribers would be affected, too, as that particular service was provided by Newsprinters. Largely, *The Guardian* reported and quoted the same reactions from across the publishing industries and political scene condemning the blockades as *The Daily Telegraph*.

Addressing both the Black Lives Matter and XR activist actions, Malik (2020) wrote for *The Guardian*: 'There is a difference between protesting against injustice and coercing people to believe what you do or to act in the way you think they should'. However, another article in *The Guardian* made an important point: 'Direct action risking arrest was always part of democracy. Protest – occasionally victorious . . . inhabits Britain's history. . . . That democratic tradition is now imperilled by threats of five-year prison terms and £10,000 fines' (Toynbee, 2020). The article was accompanied by a photograph of suffragette Emmeline Pankhurst being arrested in 1910. 'Extinction Rebellion activists, local councils, civil servants and the BBC are all viewed as barriers to absolute power', Toynbee (2020) continued, 'the wreckers running this government have lost any instinct for democratic values', as XR was praised for shining 'a searchlight on the UK's dysfunctional press – 80% owned by Rupert Murdoch and a few right-wing press barons'. The article also stressed that the Institute for Government had published a report warning that the government was 'well off track' to meet net-zero carbon emissions target by 2050 and that 'in trying to exterminate opposing views, this government has lost any sense of balance or argument' (Toynbee, 2020). Those comments accurately echoed activist's concerns in Busby's (2020) article: 'With some billionaire owners climate change sceptics, how can you expect what they write to really represent what is happening?'. A 92-year-old XR supporter who had been arrested that week explained the movement's urgency and actions:

> I don't enjoy being a nuisance, but we tried everything else, there's no sense of urgency; they're talking about 2050, but by then it will be too late to do anything. . . . It's my generation that has caused all this and we have a responsibility which I can't duck.

The article gave voice to several other protesters: one was quoted calling for ecocide to be made a crime, while an NHS doctor who had been part of an XR claimed that while activism can sometimes create a binary between 'us' and 'them', they were happy to find the XR Buddhist group which enabled participation but prevented further division. Addressing the controversy surrounding the legality of the XR actions, Dodd (2020) quoted Home Secretary Priti Patel who stated that the XR campaign was 'a shameful attack on our way of life' and that 'the very criminals who disrupt our free society must be stopped . . . together we must all stand firm against the guerrilla tactics of Extinction Rebellion'. While the article reported that the government has floated the idea of classing XR as an 'organised crime group', the police reportedly viewed XR as a non-violent group whose civil disobedience is time-consuming and costly to deal with. A senior police officer was quoted saying that XR was not an organised crime group, because part of an Organised Crime Group (OCG) definition is that they commit violence in achieving their aims 'and no one seriously suggests XR commit violence', as one activist stated:

> These powerful vested interests are the real organised criminals. They are the true threat to our democracy. And it's depressing – although no surprise – that so much of the political and media elite has jumped to their defence, and jumped at the opportunity to suppress people power and grassroots protest. We will not allow them to criminalise the noble tradition of non-violent civil disobedience.
>
> (Dodd, 2020)

Curiously, even *The Guardian* did not report the fact that the UK government had been formally warned for threatening press freedom at the same time as the Prime Minister condemned XR as a threat to press freedom. The Council of Europe had issued the Level 2 'media freedom alert' after the government blacklisted a group of investigative journalists and denied them access to information, as was reported by *The Independent* (Stone, 2020). This analysis shows that although both left and right-leaning papers largely condemned the methods used by XR, The Telegraph appeared to oppose the movement in principle, attempting to discredit it by questioning the aims of the movement, using demeaning vocabulary when describing the activists and the movement itself, paraphrasing to achieve scandalous headlines, highlighting the movement's internal issues and the lack of central control within the movement to portray it as a disorganised organisation, and comparing the activists to organised criminals who impact lives of the elderly and vulnerable. Although generally in agreement with the right-leaning papers when condemning the movement over the activists' attempt to stop the papers that express different opinions from being published, *The Guardian* called attention to the fact that protests are a necessary part of a democratic way of life. The Guardian journalists also highlighted the questions that The Telegraph chose to willfully ignore – the matter of ownership of the papers affected by the blockade, the ties among the power structures, financial investments and interests involved – as they questioned and critiqued the government that also often attempts to silence opposing opinions, only on a larger scale.

Extinction Rebellion decided to stop the distribution of the print version of several newspapers for one day and suddenly our politicians are up in arms. Where were they when our 'free press' was being bought up by billionaires?

(Malik, 2020)

When we asked the XR activist Jon Fuller to discuss the different approach and language used by the two newspapers, he affirmed that the XR activists are very much aware of the fact that the right-wing media will use attack tactics against the movement, and that approach won't change, so the focus is on starting conversations in left and centre-leaning media. Even though the right-leaning media editors are aware of the true state of the climate emergency, they stand by the fact that they need to sell papers, and their target audiences are less interested in that kind of content and expect more entertainment than actual factual news reporting, Jon said.

1.3.3 Reclaim These Streets – Sarah Everard vigil – March 2021

Reclaim These Streets started as a group of women looking to organise a vigil for Sarah Everard who was kidnapped by a policeman on her way home on the 3rd March 2020 and found murdered a week later, and it strongly echoes the sentiment and purpose of the Reclaim the Night movement founded in 1977 in response to the murder of 13 women by Peter Sutcliffe. Perhaps it is unsurprising then that some historical connotations were observed while analysing the media coverage of Sarah Everard vigil. What started as a thematic analysis of the articles published in the days surrounding the vigil that took place on the 13th March 2021 soon suggested a wider discourse and frame analysis (Cable, 2015, Edwards, 2014) of the issue. Ultimately, the vigil itself was portrayed in a positive light by *The Daily Telegraph*, *The Sunday Telegraph*, and *The Guardian*. Each article expressed support of the vigil quoting senior MPs, the Mayor of London, senior Church figures, and council leaders who urged the government and police to allow the vigil to take place, to grant the women the rights to gather to mourn together despite the COVID-19 concerns, although the public was encouraged to avoid the vigil. Police action was harshly criticised by both left-leaning and right-leaning media. However, the topic of women's safety concerns was addressed very differently.

The Daily Telegraph *and* The Sunday Telegraph

Initially, the frequently used words and themes observed in the right-leaning newspapers articles were 'fear', 'anger', and 'emotions'. The crime and violence against women were often narrated as emotional issues that take place in a reality different from that of the law and crime statistics. The Metropolitan Commissioner was quoted saying that it was 'thankfully incredibly rare for a woman to be abducted from our streets' (Evans et al., 2021). Same article said a crucial lesson to the police was that 'the service to victims and families of victims has to be approached from their reality, emotions and perceptions and not from what an individual police officer or the police establishment think they should be', stating that while the statistics may suggest that young males are more likely to be victims of violence from a stranger, 'this will not work to reassure women in the outpouring of experiences and emotions'. The article claimed that 'the commissioner in using the term abduction and the apparent circumstances of this case will have heightened those concerns and fears'. Evans et al. (2021) then argued that although many women face harassment, aggression, and unwanted sexual advances daily, the majority of this behaviour is not reported to the police, and 'some may not easily fit the definitions of what is a crime', as 'policing is driven by statistics, evidence and what can be proved, and the mindset of the police is shaped to stand away from the emotions and look at the 'facts' (Evans et al., 2021). The article posed that the attitudes and behaviours behind the harassment and assault towards women shape the low confidence that victims of those crimes have in the criminal justice system, despite there being 'a lot more female officers in police forces', while the police have to 'balance prioritising serious crimes against those day-today issues that hugely affect the lives of women'. Such issues, stated Evans et al. (2021), 'may be hard to statistically quantify', ending the article with a suggestion that those who oversee and resource police forces need to listen to and acknowledge 'the depth of anger driving the demands of women' so that conditions can be created 'where women can enjoy the liberty and safety they deserve as a basic human right'.

Another article in the same paper explored how women, including the reporter herself, had to modify their behaviours in the wake of Sarah Everard's disappearance. It looked at the lasting mental imprint of historic murder cases on women's psyche and shed light on the more detailed statistics of offences against women and the issue of reporting and prosecution of such cases, quoting the director of the Centre for Women's Justice who criticised 'a victim blaming misogynistic culture and a woefully inadequate criminal justice system' (Steafel, 2021). The article ended with the tragic number of women and girls who were killed in the days following Sarah Everard's disappearance. *The Sunday Telegraph* (Hope et al., 2021) criticised the heavy-handed tactics used by the police at the vigil and discussed the calls from across the different political parties for the Metropolitan Police Commissioner to accept the responsibility. The article briefly covered proposed measures that the government was working on or considering to tackle crimes against women; however, there was no mention of the wider societal, cultural, or educational changes required. In the article titled 'Why are we excusing violent men?' (Timothy, 2021), *The Daily Telegraph*'s columnist criticised the Metropolitan

Police Commissioner's defence of the police actions at the vigil as untenable, positioning the vigil against the 2020 Black Lives Matter protests:

> She may well say that the Covid restrictions have no exemption for vigils and protests, but the same was true when the Black Lives Matter protests first erupted. Then the police stood by – and kneeled in fact – as crowds turned violent and attacked public property.
>
> (Timothy, 2021)

The article critiqued the 'disrespectful to women and to the vulnerable and disempowered' police culture, arguing further that while men are victims of violence, women are at a disadvantage and face violence due to being the physically weaker gender that should be protected by men. Timothy highlighted the issue that many cases of violence and assault against women never reach court, and when they do, sentences are not adequate. He discussed the need for the violent offenders register and the need to 'change cultural attitudes within the police to violence against women', called for the relevant public services to understand the connection between violence and coercion, and stated that 'we need to do something about extreme and violent pornography'. But above all, he said, we need a wider cultural change to stop the perpetrators blaming the victims, 'how many thousands of men are protected by families and friends who turn a blind eye to their abusive behaviour?' (Timothy, 2021). However, even this article only skimmed the surface of the issue without addressing the deeper cultural and educational changes needed, as it reinforced the centuries-old narrative of women being physically weaker sex that needs to be protected by the dominant males.

The Guardian

Dodd and Rawlinson (2021) reported that 'many people have shared stories of the measures they feel forced to take when walking Britain's streets'. The article quoted the London mayor Sadiq Khan, who acknowledged that London's streets are not safe for women or girls:

> It's really important that people of my gender understand that. If you're a woman or a girl, your experiences of our city, in any public space . . . is very different to if you are a man or a boy, and it's really important that people like me in positions of power and influence understand that and take steps to address that.
>
> (Dodd & Rawlinson, 2021)

On the same day, Marsh (2021) wrote: 'politicians, comedians, TV stars and journalists are among hundreds of women who have shared their experiences of feeling a sense of fear when walking home alone', highlighting the scale of the problem – those affected by the issue are not a marginalised voiceless minority but real women, including those who hold prominent positions within the society. The article shared the experiences and comments of the Sky News political correspondent, the First Minister of Scotland, a Conservative MP, a Labour MP, an ITV News newsreader, a comedian and TV presenter, a joint executive director of the legal action NGO Reprieve, and others. 'Women feared this was coming', wrote Topping (2021), 'public anger, women's anger, is rising' she continued, advising that the Reclaim These Streets vigil was planned for the weekend in London, and at least nine others were scheduled to take place in other towns and cities. 'A woman dies at the hands of a man every three days', reported Topping (2021), as she discussed the Femicide Census, the global and national increase in domestic violence, rape reports, the falling number of prosecutions, statistics on homicide, and the UN Women UK survey which revealed that almost all young women have experienced sexual harassment in public places. In the article, Andrea Simon, the director of End Violence Against Women, said: 'Women's anxiety . . . is not irrational, but informed by knowledge of the violence women face on a daily basis, from micro-aggressions to murder'. Topping's article looked into the Government's failures to address the issue in the past and discussed new and proposed legislation. Farah Mazeer, Chief Executive of Women's Aid, was quoted: 'the abuse, harassment and murder of women is a reflection of systemic misogyny and sexism within society'. Addressing the issues faced by specialist refuges and minoritised women, Topping (2021) interviewed Pragna Patel from Southall Black Sisters, who suggested that the domestic abuse bill 'could not be divorced from a wider conversation about how patriarchy is embedded in state structures', which is 'a cause and consequence of gender inequality'. An article by Obordo and Otte (2021) gave voice to five women sharing their feelings when they found themselves alone in public spaces after dark. Stewart and Elgot's (2021) article addressed the challenges and actions the government was taking in the attempt to tackle the issue of violence against women and girls, and Labour leader Keir Starmer was quoted saying that the first step was to recognise the scale of violence against women and girls as not everyone understood 'how prevalent and pervasive it is' and to tackle this at the root is to 'challenge behaviours . . . there's a particular issue for men. It's very important for men to speak out on this issue'. In the same article, Labour MP Rosie Duffield was acknowledged to have spoken about her own experience of domestic abuse. *The Guardian* interviewed the organiser of the UK's first Reclaim the Night marches to get her thoughts on the issue, from raising men's awareness to calling out other men for the purpose of becoming allies, to highlighting how little has changed in societal attitudes since 1977:

> Questions are asked about how late it was, why was she alone, what was she wearing, what did she expect. . . . We should be educating boys about what men should and shouldn't do. . . . [B]oys should grow up feeling

ready to be accountable, and girls should feel able to not have to think it's their fault.

(Campbell, 2021)

Savage et al. (2021) quoted Caroline Nokes, Conservative chair of the women and equalities committee, who refused to continue to tolerate the way women including herself are treated by men and claimed that making misogyny a hate crime was a radical but necessary step. In contrast to *The Daily Telegraph* (Evans et al., 2021), *The Guardian* (O'Callaghan & Smith, 2021) questioned the way in which the Metropolitan Police chief framed Sarah Everard's disappearance and violence against women in general:

By that . . . statement the Metropolitan minimised the risk women face from men, and intentionally diminished femicide. '"Incredibly rare" should mean much more than very unusual. "Abducted from our streets" is a curious deflection. Strangers do abduct women, but they also kill women on the street, or follow them, or enter their homes. And friends, acquaintances, partners and colleagues also abduct women they know and kill them. It is also far more common to be abducted from the street and raped, attacked or sexually assaulted with impunity.

(O'Callaghan & Smith, 2021)

It is noticeable that in The Telegraph articles, the issue of violence against women and the fear arising from it was framed as one based more on emotions rather than statistics, painting the centuries-old picture of a woman as an incapable and passive being who faces violence and needs to be taken care of. The Telegraph appeared to rely on opinions and frame building without substantial evidence or reasoning for either of those, skimming over the facts and issues. *The Guardian* paid more attention to the cause and reasoning that drove the events, social and political context analysis surrounding the issues, and the government and society's mistakes, supporting reporters' claims with facts and statistics.

1.3.4   *Who decides where marginalised groups can roam?*

The disdain towards the police expressed by the media in the wake of Sarah Everard vigil raises several questions worth exploring, for example, had more male allies attended the peaceful vigil, would the framing remain the same across the different newspapers? And if it was a different (marginalised or not) group organising a peaceful vigil for one of their own, would they receive the same support from the media? Two different ways in which the violence against women was framed by the two major newspapers representing opposing political views suggest avenues for further research. First, although certain that the articles were published in response to Sarah Everard's kidnapping and murder, we cannot be sure how much coverage the issue would have received had it not been for the 'contentious episode of claim making' which suggests a double opportunity to apply the contentious politics approach (Edwards, 2014). On one hand, there were the Reclaim These Streets vigil organisers and supporters claiming their right to occupy a physical public space – Clapham Common – for a period of time, clashing with the restrictions enforced by the police. On the other hand, it mirrored in miniature the worldwide and centuries-old claim of women (and marginalised groups) to remove restrictions to their free movement and safety not only through and in physical places and spaces but also within any sites of engagement (Massey, 1994; Jones, 2005), admitting that those restrictions had been imposed by patriarchal power structures. After Sarah Everard's kidnapping, the police were telling women of London to stay in their own homes if they wanted to be safe, further heightening concerns and pressures of isolation. While the police were looking for suspects, women who lived alone had additional worries about potential new dangers of, for example, postmen or delivery drivers being a threat. As Doreen Massey (1994, p. 234) writes, historically 'respectable' women could not roam the public spaces alone not only for the reasons of socially constructed 'propriety' but also for the threat that those 'non-respectable' women who dared to wander the streets alone would have their movements restricted by male violence, and so women were excluded from the public spaces as objects of unwanted male attention and brutality.

Noting that the Reclaim These Streets and Reclaim The Night movements' message remains unchanged despite nearly half a century passing is a simple and obvious observation to make, however, it offers insight and poses a question about the long-term absence of action addressing a long-standing societal issue. Paying attention to time 'as one mode of becoming of things, events, identities, representation is . . . the only way to proceed if we want to address seriously the issue of change, a process that necessarily consumes time' (de Saint-Georges, 2005, p. 165). The lack of action and change suggests the lack of interest from existing power structures. As Massey (1994) observes, the spheres of political action, culture, and intellectual debate have been traditionally dominated by the white males, and so the conversations, behaviours within the social groups, and educational systems have formed accordingly, creating not only legal but also ideological and educational barriers to those marginalised groups that have not been included in the power structures in the past to address their issues and views. Mascia-Lees (Mascia-Lees et al., 1989, cited in Massey, 1994, p. 215) comments: 'When Western white males – who traditionally have controlled the production of knowledge – can no longer define the truth . . . their response is to conclude that there is not a truth to be discovered'. It is interesting to note that while the means and methods of communication between Reclaim These Streets and Reclaim the Night movements and activists and the media have changed and evolved in line with the technological and societal developments, more than 40 years later, the message remains the same – women are still limited to certain spaces and times of the day, or they have to face unwanted consequences.

In wider context, this applies to other movements, activist actions, and, of course, marginalised groups. Although supposedly undisputed, the right to protest often faces questions and at least some degree of backlash as soon as it moved from the theoretical realm into the physical. To what extent the public, the media, and the police are willing to welcome the disruption to the familiar routines, conversations, and places remains a question with no sole answer. As our discussion showed so far, even three different events that took place within same time frame, locality, and with very similar restrictions in place received different reactions and media framing, which highlights not only how the interests behind the media reporting and the views on different issues create different frames that get chosen to form the narratives, but also how inconsistent the media, the public, and the government can be in their approach. Very often the justification used for those inconsistencies will be the concern for public safety, public convenience, and the free speech, willingly ignoring the fact that 'the public' is not a homogenous mass. Increasing the policing of public gatherings while ignoring the concerns of marginalised groups' safety in public spaces in general raises the question of who those spaces belong to, and what is their purpose, if the power structures are willing to impose limitations on public gatherings and protests but choose inaction when it comes to granting safety of people who are most in danger. If not the people, then who own the rights to the city?

References

Adams, T. (2020) Now is the time': London's Black Lives Matter rally looks like a turning point. *The Guardian* [Online], 7 June. Available from: <www.theguardian.com/us-news/2020/jun/06/now-is-the-time-londons-black-lives-matter-rally-looks-like-a-turning-point> [Accessed 7 August 2021].

Bernays, E. (2004) *Propaganda*. New ed. New York: IG Publishing.

Bird, S., and Malnick, E. (2020) Police accused of facilitating assault on press freedom. *The Sunday Telegraph* [Online], 6 September. Available from: <https://www.telegraph.co.uk/news/2020/09/05/police-accused-offacilitating-assaulton-press-freedom/> [Accessed 7 August 2021].

Busby, M. (2020) 'Freeing the truth' – Extinction rebellion activists on their week of action. *The Guardian* [Online], 7 September. Available from: <www.theguardian.com/environment/2020/sep/07/freeing-the-truth-extinction-rebellion-activists-on-their-week-of-action> [Accessed 7 August 2021].

Cable, J. (2015) Lights, camera, direct action: The protest spectacle as media opportunity and message carrier. In: Lamond, I. R. and Spracklen, K. eds. *Protests as Events*. London: Rowman & Littlefield International, pp. 59–74.

Camber, R., Groves, J., and Brown, L. (2020) Lawless & reckless. *The Daily Maily* [Online], 8 June. Available from: <www.pressreader.com/uk/daily-mail/20200608/281492163547463> [Accessed 7 August 2021].

Campbell, L. (2021) Men must challenge other men on women's safety, campaigner says. *The Guardian* [Online], 12 March. Available from: <www.theguardian.com/uk-news/2021/mar/12/men-must-challenge-other-men-womens-safety-campaigner-al-garthwaite-sarah-everard> [Accessed 7 August 2021].

Castells, M. (2015) *Networks of Outrage and Hope: Social Movements in the Internet Age*. Cambridge: Polity Press.

Chomsky, N. (1991) *Media Control: The Spectacular Achievements of Propaganda*. New York: Seven Stories Press.

della Porta, D. (2008) Eventful protest, global conflicts. *Distinktion: Journal of Social Theory* 9(2), 27–56.

della Porta, D., Andretta., M., Mosca, L., and Reiter, H. (2006) *Globalization from below: Transnational Activists and Protest Networks*. Minneapolis: University of Minnesota Press.

de Saint-Georges, I. (2005) From anticipation to performance: Sites of engagement as process. In: Norris, S. and Jones, R. H. eds. *Discourse in Action: Introducing Mediated Discourse Analysis*. Abingdon: Routledge, pp. 155–165.

Dodd, V. (2020) Extinction rebellion 'criminals' threaten UK way of life, says Priti Patel. *The Guardian* [Online], 8 September. Available from: <www.theguardian.com/environment/2020/sep/08/extinction-rebellion-criminals-threaten-uks-way-of-life-says-priti-patel> [Accessed 7 August 2021].

Dodd, V., and Rawlinson, K. (2021) Sarah Everard suspect: Metropolitan faces inquiry over indecent exposure claim. *The Guardian* [Online], 11 March. Available from: <www.theguardian.com/uk-news/2021/mar/11/sarah-everard-suspect-met-accused-failures-alleged-indecent-exposure> [Accessed 7 August 2021].

Dowden, O. (2020) Press is a cornerstone of our precious liberties. Never take it for granted. *The Daily Telegraph* [Online], 7 September. Available from: <https://www.pressreader.com/uk/the-daily-telegraph/20200907/281694027182581> [Accessed 7 August 2021].

Edwards, G. (2014) *Social Movements and Protests – Key Topics in Sociology*. Cambridge: Cambridge University Press.

Evans, M. (2020) Protesters hurl statue of slave trader into harbour. *The Daily Telegraph* [Online], 8 June. Available from: <www.pressreader.com/uk/the-daily-telegraph/20200608/textview> [Accessed 7 August 2021].

Evans, M., Mendick, R., and Bird, S. (2021) Everard suspect 'exposed himself in restaurant'. *The Daily Telegraph* [Online], 12 March. Available from: <www.telegraph.co.uk/news/2021/03/11/sarah-everard-suspect-exposed-restaurant/?li_source=LI&li_medium=liftigniter-onward-journey> [Accessed 7 August 2021].

Extinction Rebellion (2021) XR v Murdoch: Trials begin for blockade of Broxbourne printworks [Online]. Available from: <https://extinctionrebellion.uk/2021/05/10/xr-v-mhttps://extinctionrebellion.uk/2021/05/10/xr-v-murdoch-trials-begin-for-blockade-of-broxbourne-printworks/urdoch-trials-begin-for-blockade-of-broxbourne-printworks/> [Accessed 18 August 2021].

Fawkes, J. (2007) Public relations models and persuasion ethics: A new approach. *Journal of Communication Management* 11, 313–331. https://www.researchgate.net/publication/235301820_Public_relations_models_and_persuasion_ethics_A_new_approach

Gatten, E., and Swelling (2020) Environmentalists accuse protesters of setting back action on climate change. *The Daily Telegraph* [Online], 7 September. Available from: <https://www.pressreader.com/uk/the-daily-telegraph/20200907/textview> [Accessed 7 August 2021].

Getz, D., and Ziakas, V. (2020) Shaping the event portfolio management field: Premises and integration. *International Journal of Contemporary Hospitality Management* 32(11), 3523–3544.

Herman, E. S., and Chomsky, N. (1988) *Manufacturing Consent: The Political Economy of the Mass Media*. New York: Pantheon Books.

Hope, C., Sawer, P., Steafel, E., and Bird, S. (2021) Metropolitan chief faces calls to quit as police clash with vigil women. *The Sunday Telegraph* [Online], 14 March. Available from: <www.pressreader.com/uk/the-sunday-telegraph/20210314/281487869104760> [Accessed 7 August 2021].

Iqbal, N. (2020) Climate activists accused of 'attacking free press' by blockading print works. *The Guardian* [Online], 5 September. Available from: <www.theguardian.com/environment/2020/sep/05/climate-activists-accused-of-attacking-free-press-by-blockading-print-works> [Accessed 7 August 2021].

Jones, R. H. (2005) Sites of engagement as sites of attention: Time, space and culture in electronic discourse. In: Norris, S. and Jones, R. H. eds. *Discourse in Action: Introducing Mediated Discourse Analysis*. Abingdon: Routledge, pp. 141–154.

Knapp, P. (2022) #16 Zoë Blackler and Steve Tooze on the power of the media, and its responsibility to cover the climate crisis. *Tipping Points*, Spotify [Podcast], 4 March. Available from: <https://open.spotify.com/episode/1b DSLKIpNiRfa6K8O0h97y> [Accessed 5 August 2023].

Lamond, I. R., and Spracklen, K. (2015) Introduction. In: Lamond, I. R. and Spracklen, K. eds. *Protests as Events*. London: Rowman & Littlefield International, Ltd., pp. 1–16.

Lefebvre, H. (2004) *Rhythmanalysis: Space, Time, and Everyday Life*. London: Continuum.

Lipsky, M. (1968) Protest as a Political Resource. *The American Political Science Review* 62(4), 1144–1158.

Malik, K. (2020) Persuasion, not coercion, should be the goal of BLM and Extinction Rebellion. *The Guardian* [Online], 6 September. Available from: <www.theguardian.com/commentisfree/2020/sep/06/salute-blm-and-extinction-rebellion-when-they-protest-not-when-they-coerce> [Accessed 7 August 2021].

Mars, M. M. (2013a) Forms of innovation: Product and process. In: Mars, M., Hoskinson, S. and Libecap, G. eds. *A Cross-Disciplinary Primer on the Meaning and Principles of Innovation*. Bingley: Emerald, pp. 35–49.

Mars, M. M. (2013b) Framing the conceptual meaning and fundamental principles of innovation. In: Mars, M., Hoskinson, S. and Libecap, G. eds. *A Cross-Disciplinary Primer on the Meaning and Principles of Innovation*. Bingley: Emerald, pp. 1–12.

Marsh, S. (2021) 'Always with keys out': Hundreds of women tell of fear of walking alone. *The Guardian* [Online], 11 March. Available from: <www.theguardian.com/uk-news/2021/mar/11/sarah-everard-hundreds-women-fear-walking-alone> [Accessed 7 August 2021].

Malnick, E. (2020) Extinction Rebellion facing 'organised crime' curbs. *The Sunday Telegraph* [Online], 6 September. Available from: <https://www.pressreader.com/uk/the-sunday-telegraph/20200906/textview> [Accessed 7 August 2021].

Mascia-Lees, F.E., Sharpe, P. and Ballerino Cohen, C. (1989) *The Postmodernist Turn in Anthropology: Cautions from a Feminist Perspective*. Chicago: The University of Chicago Press.

Massey, D. (1994) *Space, Place and Gender*. Cambridge: Polity Press.

McGreal, C. (2020) '"Get your knee off our necks" Sharpton delivers moving eulogy at Floyd memorial", *The Guardian*, 5 June [Online]. Available at <https://www.theguardian.com/us-news/2020/jun/04/george-floyd-memorial-minneapolis>

Mendick, R., Gatten, E., and Swerling, G. (2020) Newspapers are like Nazis, says organiser of blockade. *The Daily Telegraph* [Online], 7 September. Available from: <https://www.pressreader.com/uk/the-daily-telegraph/20200907/281676847313397> [Accessed 7 August 2021].

Murphy, E. (2020) *Arms in Academia: The Political Economy of the Modern UK Defence Industry*. London: Routledge India.

Obordo, R., and Otte, J. (2021) 'I stick to well-lit and busy areas': Women share their fears of walking alone at night. *The Guardian* [Online], 11 March. Available from: <www.theguardian.com/lifeandstyle/2021/mar/11/i-stick-to-well-lit-and-busy-areas-five-women-share-their-fears-on-walking-alone-at-night> [Accessed 7 August 2021].

O'Callaghan, C., and Smith, K. I. (2021) Cases like Sarah Everard's are not 'incredibly rare' and the police must admit it. *The Guardian* [Online]. Available from: <www.theguardian.com/society/2021/mar/14/cases-like-everards-not-incredibly-rare-police-must-admit-it> [Accessed 7 August 2021].

Olusoga, D. (2020) Britain is not America. But we too are disfigured by deep and pervasive racism. *The Guardian* [Online], 7 June. Available from: <www.theguardian.com/commentisfree/2020/jun/07/britain-is-not-america-but-we-too-are-disfigured-by-deep-and-pervasive-racism> [Accessed 7 August 2021].

Riley-Smith, B., and Sabur, R. (2020) Trump decries "terrorists" as riots sweep US. *The Daily Telegraph* [Online], 1 June. Available from: <www.pressreader.com/uk/the-daily-telegraph/20200601/textview> [Accessed 7 August 2021].

Savage, M., Graham-Harrison, E., and Tapper, J. (2021) Sarah Everard: Metropolitan defends policing of London vigil as 'necessary'. *The Guardian* [Online], 14 March. Available from: <www.theguardian.com/uk-news/2021/mar/13/sarah-everard-pressure-for-new-laws-to-curb-violence-against-women> [Accessed 7 August 2021].

Sawer, P., and Lowe, Y. (2020) UK protesters join the global outcry at George Floyd's death. *The Daily Telegraph* [Online], 7 June. Available from: <www.pressreader.com/uk/the-daily-telegraph/20200607/textview> [Accessed 7 August 2021].

Shukaitis, S. (2009a) *Imaginal Machines: Autonomy & Self-organization in the Revolutions of Everyday Life*. Brooklyn: Autonomedia.

Shukaitis, S. (2009b) *Combination Acts: Notes on Collective Practice in the Undercommons*. Brooklyn: Autonomedia.

Slawson, N., and Waterson, J. (2020) Boris Johnson accuses Extinction Rebellion of trying to limit public access to news. *The Guardian* [Online], 5 September. Available from: <www.theguardian.com/environment/2020/sep/04/extinction-rebellion-block-roads-to-murdoch-paper-print-sites> [Accessed 7 August 2021].

Steafel, E. (2021) Male violence is something we live with. Whoever we are. Wherever we go. *The Daily Telegraph* [Online], 12 March. Available from: <www.pressreader.com/uk/the-daily-telegraph/20210312/281522228839186> [Accessed 7 August 2021].

Stewart, H., and Elgot, J. (2021) Boris Johnson comes under pressure to make UK safer for women. *The Guardian* [Online], 11 March. Available from: <www.theguardian.com/uk-news/2021/mar/11/boris-johnson-comes-under-pressure-to-make-uk-safer-for-women> [Accessed 7 August 2021].

Stone, J. (2020) Council of Europe issues media freedom alert over UK government blacklisting of investigative journalists. *The Independent* [Online], 6 September. Available from: <www.independent.co.uk/news/uk/politics/press-freedom-uk-government-council-europe-alert-boris-johnson-priti-patel-a9706741.html> [Accessed 7 August 2021].

Timothy, N. (2021) Why are we excusing violent men? *The Daily Telegraph* [Online], 15 March. Available from: <www.pressreader.com/uk/the-daily-telegraph/20210315/281556588582711> [Accessed 7 August 2021].

Tominey, C. (2020) They only want press if it agrees with their agenda. *The Sunday Telegraph* [Online], 6 September. Available from: <https://www.pressreader.com/uk/the-sunday-telegraph/20200906/textview> [Accessed 7 August 2021].

Topping, A. (2021) Endemic violence against women is causing a wave of anger. *The Guardian* [Online], 11 March. Available from: <www.theguardian.com/world/2021/mar/11/endemic-violence-against-women-is-causing-a-wave-of-anger> [Accessed 7 August 2021].

Toynbee, P. (2020) It is our democratic right to protest – but this government is crushing all opposition. *The Guardian* [Online], 7 September. Available from: <www.theguardian.com/commentisfree/2020/sep/07/democratic-right-protest-government-crushing-opposition> [Accessed 7 August 2021].

Trottier, D., and Fuchs, C. (2015) Theorising social media, politics and the state: An introduction. In: Trottier, D. and Fuchs, C. eds. *Social Media, Politics and the State: Protests, Revolutions, Riots, Crime and Policing in the Age of Facebook, Twitter and YouTube*. Abingdon: Routledge, pp. 3–38.

White, M. (2016) *The End of Protest: A New Playbook for Revolution*. Toronto: Penguin Random House.

2 Protests as individual experiences

2.1 The right to and an experience of a place

When we consider the disruption that protests bring to the public and everyday lives, it is vital to understand the meaning and purpose of spaces and places – they are important aspects to discuss when analysing social movements and protests. Drawing from various authors, Venturini (2020) argues that the rights to urban spaces and cities belong to those marginalised and underrepresented, as the melting pot of people should be able to shape the city and self-manage – a vision impossible in the capitalist societies where the state powers, privatisation, and policies prevent the freedoms of making and remaking the cities and people. As Harvey (2008, p. 23) puts it, the right to the city is a type of human right, it's 'a right to change ourselves by changing the city'. Venturini (2020) believes that the concepts of the rights to the city and spatial justice should be communicated by the social movements as mobilising concepts, enabling them to reach broad audiences across the class and national limits. The idea of one's right to occupy a space and the concerns of the prevailing spatial inequality (or injustice) in towns and cities echoes Massey's (1994, p. 155) beliefs that 'places are processes' that are continuously reproduced, do not need to have boundaries, and are constructed of social relations. Defining a single identity of a place based on its (often idealised) history means drawing a boundary and 'constructing a counter position between us and them' (Massey, 1994, p. 152) in spaces where other influences such as race and gender already impact the experience of a place. Both Moore (2020) and Schupbach (2020) believe that recent Black Lives Matter protests across the world offered the perfect background for new conversations about reimagined urban spaces, if only the conversations on city development could be made truly just and democratic by taking them out of the council buildings and planning offices into the streets and affected neighbourhoods. It is worth remembering that these days, it is no longer just the physical spaces that make action, interaction, and events possible. With the digital age, online platforms brought new sites of engagement (Jones and Norris, 2005), where identities and networks develop and relationships grow.

DOI: 10.4324/9781003460640-3

On a personal level, protests create an environment where reciprocal knowledge can be developed, fostered, and exchanged through the informal networks, where friendships are made and, as demonstrated in della Porta's research (2008, p. 36), creative elements in protest events have the potential to generate experiences and memories of parties and festivals, creating similar meaningful consumer experiences as commercial events. Holbrook (Woodward & Holbrook, 2013) contends that consumer experience encompasses any and every human experience and therefore it does relate not only to the commercialised consumption of products and services but rather to all the aspects of day-to-day life, a view that 'regards consumption as a primary subjective state of consciousness with a variety of symbolic meanings, hedonic responses, and esthetic criteria' (Holbrook & Hirschman, 1982, p. 132). Event management and experiential marketing scholars have long been exploring the varying feelings and meanings involved in 'consuming' and sharing experiences based on the theories of multiplicity of individual's (or consumer's) selves, individual's search for belonging and happiness, and the need and anticipation of the extraordinary and participating in events that become life-changing experiences (Caprariello & Reis, 2012; Bahl & Milne, 2010; Wood & Moss, 2015; Carù & Cova, 2003; Bhattacharjee & Mogilner, 2014; Green, 2016). Carù and Cova (2007) separate specific sequences within a consumer experience, highlighting the consumer's need for finding familiar anchorage points, observation, and discovery of something new, and the importance of attributing a meaning to the situation or experience, but they also stressed the role of service elements relating to those sequences. This experience of service, often associated with commercial events, is also found in protest events. White (2016) recalls how the free kitchens provided superb meals to the participants at the Occupy Wall Street event, while excellent organisation of the space, clean paths, great service, and staffing both contributed to the appeal to passers-by and helped to create a sense of community.

The strength of emotions evoked when participating in protests, the sense of solidarity, creation of joint narratives, and rituals attached to the experience cement the sense of belonging; however, even the negative emotionally charged experiences such as confronting the police, other citizens, or groups in the protest spaces can help strengthen the feeling of collective identity and community (della Porta, 2008). As is the case in commercial consumer events, rituals and consumers' individual rites are exceptionally important to the outcome of the consumption experience, where subjective operations occurring during the process of immersion in the experience are difficult to measure, manage, and anticipate, as consumption provokes sensations and emotions that touch on the participant's search for identity (Carù & Cova, 2003, 2007). While some messages and slogans have the potential to be misunderstood, shared cultural symbols and traditions can involve unknowing onlookers and break the awkwardness, forming 'a moment where the passivity of the crowd perhaps is broken, and the nature of the space is transformed' (Shu-kaitis, 2009a, p. 112). The spectacle, the melody, words, and memories con-nect, and new mobile and affective spaces are created through the protest's performativity, where the 'ideas, memories, histories, cultures and stories' mix and 'rage blends with joy; dislocation replaced by emerging, momen-tary worlds' (Shukaitis, 2009a, p. 113), as new experiences and personal and collective narratives are created (Holbrook & Hirschman, 1982; Woodward & Holbrook, 2013). It is then, through the networks and workings of time and space (Jones, 2005), emerging new world narratives, participants, and ideas (Latour, 2005) that are believed to be real, that action takes place, and real consequences are brought into being (Goldfarb, 2001; Shukaitis, 2009b). According to Jones (2005, p. 153), sites of engagement are junctions where social practices, individuals and their histories, ideas, plans, social identities, relationships, and architectural or software designs and discourses converge. There exists a continuously changing and evolving connection between the social imaginary and various forms of self-organisation and interactions and relations that continue to both express and develop through this relationship (Shukaitis, 2009a, p. 76).

2.2 Organising a protest during COVID-19 pandemic

COVID-19 pandemic and the lockdowns of 2020–2021 created a unique emo-tionally charged climate for the protests to take place. Jamie Klingler, one of the founders of Reclaim These Streets, the group formed to organise the Sarah Everard vigil, agrees:

> We were in lockdown, police were telling women if they wanted to be safe to stay in their own homes and then it came out it was one of them – just the anger. . . . I hadn't hugged anyone, I hadn't seen my friends, I lived alone. . . . The isolation of it all and then knowing it could have been me.

All this, she says, prompted her to organise the vigil, and it was very organic and unexpected, but she felt the women needed a space to gather safely and to share the grief. Jamie's event management background and understanding publicity played a vital role, too:

> 'I knew how to make a safe space for women, it was much less political. I knew I could go to the police; I could go to the council, I could make it safe, that's why I said I would do a vigil and that's why I was well placed to do so – because of my events management training,' said Jamie, 'that is my background – it's much more in amplification and publicity around the events and ideas. The company that I started with was Creative Influence Alliance which is about experiential marketing.'

Jamie recalled the first online meeting with the group of women that were to become Reclaim These Streets as a very organic response to what was happening (Wayne Couzens' arrest and Sarah Everard's remains being found) as they hadn't physically met each other and didn't know each other. She says that if any of them had been 'anarchists', they wouldn't have worked together, but they all had different experiences, and the combination of those worked perfectly to make the event happen. Two of the organisers were counsellors who volunteered to handle the health and safety of the event, and they were all concerned about the risks and safety:

> Where we were having it [Clapham Common] was really intentional. It was in such a wide space. I had a thousand electric tea lights, we were going to spread them out 2 meters apart from each other, our high-viz had a track and trace codes on the back of them so people could check in when they got there, we had a Lost Child tent, we were also going to have Good Samaritans and rape counsellors there, if people were finding it traumatic, we had people who were going to walk attendees back to the bus stops.

She said that in preparation for the vigil, they had consulted the Council, local police, and Public Health England to maximise the safety measures.

Organising the vigil and joining other women to start Reclaim These Streets was the first time that Jamie was involved in social activism, too. She says when people ask about her qualifications to organise the vigil and to campaign for women's safety, her response is simple: 'being a woman and for the whole of my adult life being objectified, touched and against my will being subjected to abuse'. 'I have been attacked for it and they're right', she continued,

> [W]hy did it take a white woman to be killed for me to feel this way and step up and be noticed, but I think we were in the third section of lockdown, we were so tired, we were so scared, we've gone through two cycles of being alone and then this happened. And for her to be wearing a bright jumper, and for her to have called her boyfriend.

One of the most difficult aspects of this case, emotionally, especially for women, was that Sarah Everard had done everything every woman is told to do to stay safe: she phoned her partner, she walked a well-lit street, she wore bright clothing, and, as it was discovered in the end, her only mistake was to trust a policeman. Jamie comes from Philadelphia, where, she says, people are raised to not trust the police, but she knows the attitudes are very different in the UK: 'Any single one of us could have been in that car. None of us would have gotten away from him. It was so heart breaking that he just plucked her off the street'. Perhaps that was the reason why the media and the public united in the support for the vigil, and Jamie agrees. She says there was no question about support – the whole country was behind Reclaim These Streets, and for the first time men were starting and joining conversations that were only had taken place privately before. Many women shared one observation, and Jamie concurred: 'What my [male] friends didn't understand is how often it was happening. We don't get harassed once a week – it's very pervasive, you're constantly thinking of how to prepare and how to keep yourself safe'.

Every organiser of Reclaim These Streets had different experiences and strengths, so Jamie, with her understanding of publicity, was chosen as one of the spokeswomen for the movement to stand in front of the camera. She did over 400 interviews, although she'd never really been in front of a TV camera before, and she made sure she was available. The interviews had been hard hitting, but Jamie said she likes sparring. She wrote for every newspaper, including *The House Magazine*, a publication for MPs and peers, that she had been told everyone in Westminster read:

> I'm not registered with any political party; I've met with various MPs – it isn't a political thing, what I want is women to stay alive. I wasn't asking for male curfews or anything like that, so male conservative hosts agreed with me. . . . I don't find as much value going to the shows that are listened to by people who agree with me, I'd much rather go on conservative shows, and most interviews had been very welcoming and agreeable to what I had to say.

One of the big concerns that Jamie mentioned a couple of times in our conversation was that discussions about Sarah Everard's murder and the circumstances surrounding it highlighted the fact that the voices and experiences of black women, especially involving the police, had been ignored. Many had repeated 'We've been saying this and writing about this for years, you just never noticed'; she said and agreed that that is the area where her privilege came out, as she expected the police to help.

> Had the police just let us get on with it, we would have had 5 or 6 camera crews there and gotten back to the normal life. What happened there was by trying to cancel it they brought so much more publicity and still thought they could squash us down – them bringing publicity by trying to cancel it poured gasoline and it got bigger, and bigger.

The public and the media agreed that police actions were hard to understand.

> Harriet Harman [Labour MP] wrote a letter to Cressida Dick [Commissioner of Metropolitan police at the time] on the 11 or 12th March, she wrote publicly to say not only did we have a reasonable excuse to do the vigil, but she would be attending with her daughter. Harriet is not only an

MP, she's also a barrister of incredible criminal standing. And to be taken to High Court . . . when all we wanted was a moment of silence.

Jamie told us of the unfolding of events that took place within a few days before the vigil:

I tweeted about the vigil, I was put in touch with Reclaim These Streets women – we became Reclaim These Streets that night – the next morning we found out we won't be allowed the vigil, we found out Human Rights lawyer – on Twitter. And then we had to raise £30,000 that night since we were taken to High Court on Friday, we raised approximately £37,000 in 45 minutes. That was our barometer to know whether people wanted us to fight the Metropolitan.

More than two years on, Jamie still finds the way the Metropolitan police treated Reclaim These Streets impossible to comprehend, saying that the condescension and antagonistic behaviour continued for a long time:

Threatening we would be prosecuted, and fined. And then they mocked us. In court they told us there was no ban on the protests and asked us to pay the fees. The High Court . . . said this should never have gotten to court. But while we were negotiating with Scotland Yard afterwards, they sent out a press release saying [the vigil] was illegal. They just mocked and ridiculed us the entire time, and I couldn't get over the fact they had women do it every single time they did it.

Jane Connors (who was Metropolitan's lead for COVID-19 enforcement) ordered Reclaim These Streets to cancel the vigil or be prosecuted. Jamie claims they had pointed out to the police that in the event of the vigil being cancelled, people would still gather, only without the planned safety measures in place, and that other events were being planned across the country. The High Court ruled that the planned event was not illegal, but recommended that the police should inform the organisers of the legal requirements to ensure the vigil didn't breach any guidelines, which the police refused to do. Not wanting to risk facing arrests and fines, the organisers announced that the vigil would not go ahead, and none of the Reclaim These Streets organisers attended the gathering that still took place. Jamie mused:

There was an article in *The Guardian* after it happened that there was a memo from Priti Patel saying 'shut it down at any cost'. . . . It was so badly handled, and then having them kneel on Patsy [one of the women who was arrested] after the vigil. The headlines in the media the following day were so critical of the police. And if the Daily Mail is so critical of the police.

We met with Cressida Dick, and when asked what she would have done knowing what she knew then, she said 'Absolutely nothing', even after the publication of police kneeling on Patsy. I asked her to wave the fines for the five women arrested, she said absolutely not.

A year later, in 2022, the High Court held that the police acted unlawfully in preventing Reclaim These Streets from organising the vigil, because they failed to give proper consideration to the rights to freedom of expression and assembly, protected under Articles 10 and 11 of the European Convention on Human Rights (ECHR).

2.3 The impact of activism on individual's safety and well-being

Protest and activism in general can hold a lot of emotion, which encompasses anything from being passionate about the cause to worrying about personal safety at the event. In the example of Sarah Everard vigil, there is again the concern of the issue of women's safety being framed as an emotional rather than factual worry, as we have witnessed in the news and opinion pieces published by the right-leaning media. This has a potential to create additional consideration for the activists not wanting to reinforce harmful media narratives. And even if the media and public may be supportive of the event, it doesn't mean that the impact and repercussions won't last a long time after the end of the protest. Jamie Klinger reflects:

I was ok to get arrested, but there were women who worried about their immigration status, their parliamentary pass, there were all these concerns. We said if we raised £37,000 in 45 minutes, we will raise £90,000, for our fines, but there were 31 other satellite vigils that were going to take place, and we thought if all those women also get fined, that's £320,000 – if we pivot and raise money, we will give the money to help women's lives, not to fund the police. We raised £550,000 – which is unheard of, for an organisation that didn't exist before, one that we put together to organise the vigil. But the police backed us into the corner and we raised money, and we kept the police reform and women's safety on the front pages for nearly two years.

However, this comes with a cost. 'When it was happening, all the adrenaline, all was going. But a year later, I was reading the court papers while I was in America visiting my family, and I didn't get out of bed for three days', remembers Jamie Klingler.

We spoke to Peter Knapp, the host of 'Tipping points' podcast, an Imperial College London research postgraduate and a member of Scientists for Extinction Rebellion and other activist groups, who is very aware of the toll activism can take on a person's mental well-being. According to Peter, a lot of activists join movements never having had therapy before, and a lot of them realise they can't cope, which makes them see therapy as a crucial aspect, although there are no formal provisions or financing for it in Extinction Rebellion. However, Peter shared that Just Stop Oil movement is more set up to offer structured mental health support as their actions are much more disruptive, and an activist may end up standing in front of a stadium of hostile people or be taken off the street by the police while facing aggression from the public, so another level of therapy is essential. Although Just Stop Oil has more structured support in terms of mental health aid, Extinction Rebellion has local groups where activists can discuss how to deal with things, although it's up to the individuals to organise social and support groups if they need further help. Peter himself started scientists' social and support group that can be facilitated to talk if people are struggling or unable to cope with certain things. Both movements acknowledge the importance of training and reassurance. Extinction Rebellion has protest training for those who are to attend action, and it is mainly focused on activists' rights, what to do if one gets arrested, and how to avoid it (if one needs to avoid arrest), said Peter. However, when there is action, it is always, and it is made very clear, stressed Peter, an option to step away. If a person said they could help in some critical way, and then in the final moment they need to step away – it's encouraged, because everyone knows there can be a perceived pressure to commit when an individual is involved with something. 'There is a significant amount of reassurance that you can step away at any point, even once an action has started', reassured Peter.

Although participating in activism and bringing the change can be incredibly rewarding, meaningful, and worthwhile, it is important to be aware that it isn't an easy road. Some people get involved in activism because they may feel that they have no other choice, perhaps being driven to action by certain living conditions and experiences; and others may see it as a worthwhile and rebellious outlet or a personal challenge they are willing to take. The impact that any form of activism may have on mental and physical health, the strain on relationships, and even the danger to activists' safety should not go without consideration, and in the next chapter, we will further explore the impact that activism may have on one's identity and life.

References

Bahl, S. and Milne, G.R. (2010), "Talking to Ourselves: A Dialogical Exploration of Consumption Experiences", *Journal of Consumer Research*, Vol. 37, pp. 176–195.

Bhattacharjee, A. and Mogilner, C. (2014), "Happiness from Ordinary and Extraordinary Experiences", *Journal of Consumer Research*, Vol. 41, pp. 1–17.

Caprariello, P.A. and Reis, H.T. (2012), "To Do, to Have, or to Share? Valuing Experiences Over Material Possessions Depends on the Involvement of Others", *Journal of Personality and Social Psychology*, Vol. 104 No. 2, pp. 199–215.

Carù, A. and Cova, B. (2003), "Revisiting Consumption Experience: A More Humble But Complete View of the Concept", *Marketing Theory*, Vol. 3 No. 2, pp. 267–286.

Carù, A. and Cova, B. (Eds.) (2007), Chapter 1: Consuming Experience: An Introduction. In: *Consuming Experience*. London: Routledge.

Della Porta, D. (2008), "Eventful Protest, Global Conflicts", *Distinktion: Journal of Social Theory*, Vol. 9 No. 2, pp. 27–56.

Goldfarb, J.C. (2001), "1989 and the Creativity of the Political", *Social Research*, Vol. 68 No. 4, pp. 993–1010.

Green, B. (2016), "I Always Remember That Moment: Peak Music Experiences as Epiphanies", *Sociology*, Vol. 50 No. 2, pp. 333–348.

Harvey, D. (2008), "The Right to the City", *New Left Review*, Vol. 53, pp. 23–40.

Holbrook, M.B. and Hirschman, E.C. (1982), "The Experiential Aspects of Consumption: Consumer Fantasy, Feelings and Fun", *Journal of Consumer Research*, Vol. 9 No. 2, pp. 132–140.

Jones, R.H. (2005), Sites of Engagement as Sites of Attention: Time, Space and Culture in Electronic Discourse. In: Norris, S. and Jones, R. H. eds. *Discourse in Action: Introducing Mediated Discourse Analysis*. Abingdon: Routledge, pp. 141–154.

Jones, R.H. and Norris, S. (2005), Discourse as Action/Discourse in Action. In: Norris, S. and Jones, R. H. eds. *Discourse in Action: Introducing Mediated Discourse Analysis*. Abingdon: Routledge, pp. 3–14.

Latour, B. (2005), *Reassembling the Social*. Oxford: Oxford University Press.

Massey, D. (1994), *Space, Place, and Gender*. Oxford: Polity Press.

Moore, D.L. (2020), Urban Spaces and the Mattering of Black Lives. In: Griffin, T.L., Cohen, A. and Maddox, D. eds. *The Just City Essays: 26 Visions for Urban Equity, Inclusion and Opportunity*. New York: The J. Max Bond Center, pp. 18–20.

Schupbach, J. (2020), Why Design Matters. In: Griffin, T.L., Cohen, A. and Maddox, D. eds. *The Just City Essays: 26 Visions for Urban Equity, Inclusion and Opportunity*. New York: The J. Max Bond Center, pp. 88–90.

Shukaitis, S. (2090a), *Imaginal Machines: Autonomy & Self-organization in the Revolutions of Everyday Life*. Brooklyn: Autonomedia.

Shukaitis, S. (2009b), *Combination Acts: Notes on Collective Practice in the Undercommons*. Brooklyn: Autonomedia.

Venturini, F. (2020), *Reconceptualising the Right to the City and Spatial Justice Through Social Ecology*. [Online] Available from: <http://trise.org/2020/11/08/reconceptualising-the-right-to-the-city-and-spatial-justice-through-social-ecology/> [Accessed 28 May 2021].

White, M. (2016), *The End of Protest: A New Playbook for Revolution*. Toronto: Penguin Random House.

Wood, E.H. and Moss J. (2015), "Capturing Emotions: Experience Sampling at Live Music Events", *Arts and the Market*, Vol. 5 No. 1, pp. 45–72.

Woodward, M.N. and Holbrook, M.B. (2013), "Dialogue on Some Concepts, Definitions and Issues Pertaining to 'Consumption Experiences'", *Marketing Theory*, Vol. 13 No. 3, pp. 323–344.

3 Organising events of dissent

3.1 Sites of engagement

Regardless of how the protests may be portrayed by the media and perceived by the bystanders, they tend to create a rich composition of relationships for those who get involved: through the release of social energies; new intensities and meanings being created and shared through various symbols, images, and sounds; writings on the walls; and stories retold (Shukaitis, 2009a). The decision to participate in protests does not occur in social isolation, and positive correlations between active engagement and political efficacy have been discussed for several decades (Van Stekelenburgh & Klandersmans, 2013). Putnam (1993, pp. 1–2) proposes the concept of 'social capital', which refers to 'features of social organization, such as networks, norms and trust, that facilitate coordination and cooperation for mutual benefit'. Before the Internet, when information wasn't as readily and widely available, those caring for a cause sought to be part of an organisation, or a social movement, as the organisation would play a role of an 'information-clearing house' (Shukaitis, 2009b, p. 61). But the Internet gifted people new powers. Extinction Rebellion activist Jon Fuller says that now, younger people tend to come to reach the movement attracted through social media – they see posts about what is happening and want to get involved.

Nearly two decades ago, Jones (2005, p. 143) suggested that people do not actually reside in one space, but occupy various built, geographical, political, and personal spaces at a time, and 'cyberspace' is just another one to add to the list, where actions occur not 'in' or 'at' but 'as' sites of engagement. He introduced five kinds of overlapping spaces towards which Internet users can direct their attention: the physical spaces in which they are using technology, virtual spaces created by the interfaces they use to communicate (chat rooms, web pages, social media platforms), relational spaces created by the 'state of talk' between participants that do not exist in the physical realm but are often referred to as 'here', actual screen spaces upon which users arrange various elements, and 'third spaces' which are not inhabited by the participants but referred to in their interactions (streets, squares, shops, etc), often as potential sites of future engagement (Jones, 2005, p. 144). There is potential for yet

DOI: 10.4324/9781003460640-4

other forms of space, 'the capacity to imagine a space outside this world . . . becomes an imaginal space from which it becomes possible to begin building it in the present' (Shukaitis, 2009a, p. 79). Blodgett and Tapia (2011) propose a new concept of digital protestainment, which occurs when participants engage in protest in a digital environment, while technology blurs the boundaries between protest, work, entertainment, and play, suggesting that in virtual worlds, even game environments can be used to reach new audiences and organise collective action. Peter Knapp, a member of Scientists for Extinction Rebellion, agrees that a lot of activist community development happened during COVID-19 lockdown, and it happened online. People got connected and established that connection in a way that was available at the time. That has allowed for the activism to become much more accessible, especially in the rural areas; however, while online activism can be powerful and empowering, it may also mean that when the protest action is taking place, there will be sometimes a different group of people who will be physically present. Both Jon and Peter say that a lot of Extinction Rebellion action takes place in London, as that is where the government and newspaper offices are, and there is a group of people who are more local to London and have signed up to take part in action, so frequently the news reports will have images of the same people attending the protests. Peter Knapp says this may give the wrong impression of a same group of people who do everything. However, the reality is there is a large number of people who do all the work, such as designing the leaflets, the fonts, or colour schemes; do social media posts; provide scientific scrutiny of messaging; or contact the journalists. It can all be done remotely, and therefore it can be done anywhere. The higher retention and higher involvement, he suggests, are evident when people have had an opportunity at some stage to be involved in person. He also believes that the people who get involved from the remote areas are far fewer in number partially because it seems that one has a higher chance to get involved in activism when they meet people in person, and the output and frequency of their involvement are somewhat lesser than those who do it in person.

At the beginning, freed from the narratives spread by the traditional media, from state-controlled and enforced views and opinions, online platforms provided people with the freedom to express their thoughts and the opportunity to come together without the need to physically travel. New information, ideas, and plans were shared, developed, and established and events were organised, allowing people to form friendships and movements, before they even met (Castells, 2015). Reclaim These Streets was the perfect example of a movement formed, and an event organised, before the organisers ever got to meet in person. In conversation, Jamie Klinger – one of the organisers of the Sarah Everard vigil – said:

The scariest part for me is that none of it would have happened without Twitter. I tweeted about the vigil, I was put in touch with Reclaim These

Streets women – we became Reclaim These Streets that night – the next morning we found out we won't be allowed [the vigil], we found our Human Rights lawyer – on Twitter. And then we had to raise £30,000 that night since we were taken to High Court on Friday, and we raised approximately £37,000 in 45 minutes.

We witness that not only has the Internet created new sites of engagement, but also the applications that people use have become so inbuilt in their practices and practices of the communities, shaping the norms of interaction and identity, that the new patterns and ways of operating have become part of the user's body and the mind (Jones, 2005, p. 152).

3.2 Building and rebuilding of identity and community

Social identity and connection with social groups are accepted means to enhance well-being, and Foster (2019) suggests a possibility that activism might also strengthen the *protective qualities of social identity* through a process where the discrimination or exclusion for belonging to a certain group (based on gender, ethnicity, sexuality, etc.) would increase the sense of social identity of those participating in social activism. However, it is important to understand how being part of an existing pattern of networks, connections, and composition within a social movement can pose a risk of limitation to further self-expansion, development, and creativity. Once collective problems are individualised and the network logic inhabits the mind, it may become difficult to see the possibilities, contacts, and narratives that exist outside of that collective identity (Shukaitis, 2009a, p. 176). On the flip side, some people may struggle to find their true identity and form meaningful connections outside of those movements or communities. Jon Fuller, from Extinction Rebellion, believes that only a minority of people have a strong sense of obligation; however, once people find their local groups and get involved, there is a lot to be said about meeting like-minded people and finding the sense of belonging and solidarity. Generally, he says, people rarely feel able to have conversations about their concerns, such as those associated with the climate emergency, with their neighbour on the street. Finding a community of people who share those same concerns serves a deeper purpose and may be truly empowering. Jon Fuller suggests that once people join the movement, there is, initially, a steep learning curve as they learn what media does not report on (e.g. the actual extent of the climate and ecological emergency), yet, through joint action and conversation, there comes hope that not everything is lost.

A common assumption that the digital networks provide an accessible and inclusive public sphere, a space of activist opportunities, empowerment, and digital enclosure omits the fact that those shared spaces of 'increased visibility and connectivity' may also create new forms of exclusion depending on resources, skills, and age (Fotopoulos, 2014) and, depending on the platforms and mediums used, 'to isolate even while connecting' (Ling, 2004, cited in Gerbaudo, 2012, p. 135). The absence of existence in a common time, framework, or spatial proximity may prevent individuals from finding their communalities, collective positions, and identities (Shukaitis, 2009a, pp. 178–180). It is important to understand the risk of basing common position and grounds for struggle on the assumption that shared technical composition of a movement or labour equals shared political composition, where different backgrounds, different social values assigned to the different members, and different access to forms of social power must be recognised to understand the true connected position of the movement (Shukaitis, 2009a, pp. 183–184). Gerbaudo (2018, p. 750) argues that social media is able to focus the attention of otherwise dispersed people, providing gathering spaces where 'the atoms of the dispersed social networks could be re-forged into a new political community, into an 'online crowd' of partisan supporters'. In the analysis of 15-M protests, demonstrations, and occupations against austerity policies in Spain in 2011, Gerbaudo quotes Castells, who was present at one of the protest camps, stating that the movement was possible due to the system of 'mass self-communication', while other people involved in the organisation of the protests referred to the 'networked brain' and 'connected intelligences' (Gerbaudo, 2012, p. 77). Gerbaudo proposes that the focus should be shifted to analyse why protests had not occurred before, proposing two reasons: a lot of activists who participated in the 15-M movement admitted that they felt incapable of voicing their discontent and chose to Immerse themselves in the pleasures of the Spanish nightlife instead, highlighting the inability of existing institutions and organisations to become a 'focal point in the mobilisation of emerging popular demands' (Gerbaudo, 2012, p. 78). The second reason being the stigmatisation of public gatherings by the state and the media following the worker strikes where newspapers and TV presented participants as criminals just for using their right to protest. Such stigmatisation of public gatherings affected subcultural practices and youth sociability, claims Gerbaudo (2012), explaining the reluctance and lack of focus to organise protests before the 15-M.

3.3 The personal journey and the process of becoming an activist

Peter Knapp from Extinction Rebellion wants to make it very clear that becoming an activist is a process which requires a person to refrain from 'diving head first in too deep'. He explained that every step takes time: it takes time to have conversations, to process the change, to process one's own grief of their own future, and to grieve the loss of freedom to travel the world by flying for example, when one realises there is something they can no longer do – they have to grieve that, and when individuals recognise their privilege, it can be really difficult to process. Peter gives an example of some people coming to activism from the families where maybe racism or homophobia were accepted and jokes were made, and when those people come into an activist group where everyone is using their own pronouns, people may feel they are worlds apart. By joining activist communities without any preparation, individuals may not feel warmly welcomed because they still have attitudes that people don't want in the activism groups, and that can be difficult. Peter suggests that a good solution would be to have different levels of activism groups: one would join the first group where people are still early on in their journey, and it would allow a person to become an activist without all the guilt and threat to their identity. And when they feel they no longer belong in that group – there's another one to join. Such an approach, in Peter's opinion, would make it easier for people to get into activism. He recalls that when he joined Extinction Rebellion in 2019, he still had a lot of ideas that were 'wrong', and so he was being challenged so much that he felt he was losing his identity. Peter says he also lost trust, and he felt that everyone he had trusted – his parents, his family, his teachers, his government – they all let him down by leading him to believe everything was going to be all right. When he joined the activist group and realised the future wasn't as bright as he had been told, he lost faith in all those people, and, more importantly, he lost who he thought he had been and what he was going to do. 'It felt horrible – you crash, and lose the sense of identity, and you don't trust anyone – that happened to me'. Peter understands that activism can be really difficult to get into – people go into it hard because they think so much needs to change, and they feel they have to get involved to the fullest extent they possibly can. But the individual attitudes and where they are on the personal journey may not be quite there yet. A person may learn at one trajectory, but their emotional adaptability may be on the other one, said Peter, and the more one gets involved, the bigger the disparity between what a person knows they need to do and how much they feel capable of doing. When those two things get further and further apart, one may lose the sense of identity, and they can feel dejected. And this is a big concern, stresses Peter – people get involved in activism, but they don't have the emotional tools to deals with it, and they don't have the emotional maturity. He believes capitalism has a lot to answer for as he claims that 'capitalism has kept people like children, really'. To help with the journey, a person may need support.

Although it isn't very often talked about, activists tend to help and provide therapy-like help to each other, so support is an important aspect of being within an activist community. Although peer and community support is significant, specialised help must receive more focus, and researchers agree that

> people in diverse settings experience intersecting forms of stigma that influence their mental and physical health and corresponding health behaviours. As different stigmas are often correlated and interrelated, the health impact of intersectional stigma is complex, generating a broad range of vulnerabilities and risks.
>
> (Turan et al., 2019, n.p.)

In her article about *vicarious racism* – a concept explaining that racism influences individuals even if they are not the target of racism – Heard-Garris (2021) writes that in the age of smartphones and social media, the experiences of marginalised groups are more difficult to deny, as the video and photographic evidence can be rapidly circulated and spread. 'While social media shares have been authoritative and effective tools of present-day social movements, they serve as a relevant avenue of vicarious racism'; however, activism can be a significant and productive response to such experiences:

> [A]ctivism is unique in that, it may help create change for the individual participating in the activism but also allow society to reap those same benefits so that Black Lives Matter will not be a tagline but a societal principle.
>
> (Heard-Garris, 2021, n.p.)

While many will agree that social activism paves the way for positive changes, there remain parts of society who do not welcome the change. *The Independent* (Dearden, 2020, n.p.) reported that in the wake of a backlash against Black Lives Matter protests, British far right had become more openly racist and extreme, attacking the police and journalists at the Black Lives Matter UK protests as 'some protesters appeared to perform Nazi salutes, . . . making "white power" gestures and shouting: "Why don't you go back to Africa?"'. Days after the Black Lives Matter protests, the far-right ideology supporters held publicity stunts across the country while holding 'white lives matter' banners, as they claimed that 'native British' people were being eradicated (Dearden, 2020). Many social movements, while being unable to provide free therapy, will direct the activists to the sources where relevant help can be found. For example Black Minds Matter UK is a registered charity set up to provide culturally relevant therapy for Black people in the UK. Jamie Klingler told us that provisions had been made to have rape counsellors at Sarah Everard's vigil to aid those who may have needed specialist support. Peter Knapp mentioned the name of Caroline Hickman, a lecturer at the University of Bath in social work and climate psychology, psychotherapist, and a researcher focused on eco-anxiety and distress about the climate and ecological crisis in children and young people globally. She was one of the founders of the Climate Psychology Alliance (not to be confused with the Climate Psychiatry Alliance) which offers therapy for people who need their therapist to understand the climate crisis.

Closely related to individual's well-being is the problem of online hate. Often, digital platforms and social media blur the distinction between political and personal statements and, while encouraging free speech and often anonymous participation, create a breeding ground for intentionally harmful, upsetting, and diminishing speech. Online hate has become an everyday phenomenon that can be observed in many social media conversations. Even when social media platforms are willing to stop hateful speech and conduct, the scale and speed at which online abuse can spread make it difficult to regulate and tackle. In an attempt to reinforce their attempts and strengthen their policies on hateful speech and conduct, Facebook and Twitter partnered with NGOs and launched initiatives to tackle the rise of abusive behaviour. Published in May 2021, UK government's Online Safety Bill placed a duty of care on online platforms to keep their users safe; however, the root of the problem remains – social media platforms' business model is based on an increased revenue from advertising being linked to engagement, which essentially encourages the amplification of divisive content through the use of algorithms and allows abusers to remain anonymous, giving them protection from consequences (Moynihan, 2021). In addition to publicly posted hate speech, an activist may face attacks through private messages, email, or phone. Social media platforms often remain unwilling or too slow to make a distinction between free speech and hate speech online, leaving activists and allies to form their own initiatives to challenge online vitriol (Kemekenidou, 2020) or to find their own coping mechanisms.

3.4 Digital participation

Closely related to collective identity is the concept of solidarity, accomplished when an individual's emotions are made collective, when feelings of affection and compassion among group members are reciprocated, and when individuals feel the obligation to care about others, especially members of the same group (Stewart & Schultze, 2019). Although those emotions may be more difficult to experience without the physical engagement and spatial proximity to the other members of the movement, technology-enabled protests and social media activism enable different forms of solidarity. Stewart and Schultze (2019) propose new notions of imagined and situated solidarity. Imagined solidarity is experienced when anonymous activists post images or videos online of their symbolic actions that are recognised and have meaning to other activists, but due to the activists' anonymity, the solidarity and collective identity are largely left to the imagination. Situated solidarity is experienced when regular collective action with physical presence happens among activists who may carry out symbolic actions or carry symbolic attributes of the movement, sharing evidence of their experiences and actions through their personal social media accounts, providing 'richness of insight into the actual protest situation' and creating conditions for solidarity motivated by shared emotions, for example anger for mistreatment of an individual or empathy for others (Stewart & Schultze, 2019, p. 2). Although the Internet provides both the enhancement and base for online activism, critics agree that the increased use of technology in online-based activism casts doubt on the viability of generating solidarity. The Internet enables users to hide their identities, offers occasional participation which indicates a weak sense of mutual obligation and a lack of commitment, and creates opportunities for performative behaviours such as pressing the 'like' button or signing an online petition – actions that make one feel good about themselves but have little impact (Stewart & Schultze, 2019; Foster, 2019). Other academics (Dennis, 2018; Madison & Klang, 2020) disagree, stating that this view overlooks the importance of micro-level changes at the individual level in terms of their political participation, attitudes, and behaviours that in given time may result in broader changes, while to those living under repressive regimes, online activism may stimulate offline activism (Greijdanus et al., 2020). Jon from Extinction Rebellion agrees, as he believes that only minority of people have a strong sense of obligation; however, local and interest groups for the Extinction Rebellion activists play an important role – there is a lot to be said about meeting like-minded people who share the same concerns and worries and feeling the sense of solidarity. When asked about online solidarity and actions that some may consider performative, Peter Knapp shifted focus to the concept of value. He believes the reason people donate is another issue around capitalism and that the understanding of value in our society is warped – value is seen as how much one earns, how much they have, and how they are perceived. That means people feel that by giving money, they are giving value. Peter argues that some movements, like XR, do not need any money except for paying the legal fees, and when that happens, they raise money specifically for it. If we don't factor in the money for printing costs of banners, activism doesn't cost money – 'it's not about how much you have, it's about getting boots on the ground', he says. Another interesting trend observed by Peter are people who get involved with activist groups but then become what he calls 'lurkers'. Those people join movements' WhatsApp groups, or other groups, but never participate in conversations nor action. Peter says many groups may have hundreds of people in them, but only a very small number would participate in any conversation. He wonders why people find themselves in that spot. Is it 'token' presenteeism? Perhaps. Why do people join and remain in those groups if they are not contributing? Perhaps some people feel mere presence and witnessing other activists' conversations absolve them from the guilt.

Reflecting on her own experiences as a feminist activist, Kemekenidou (2020, p. 235) states that while effective activism on social media is based around spreading and sharing information, she strongly believes that 'supporting statements, petitions or movements online, or liking a sharepic with a political message does not make one an activist'. She suggests using three levels of connection for defining fields of activism on social media, a concept proposed by Meredith Clark of the University of Texas, which Kemekenidou (2020, pp. 235–236) summarises as: personal community, thematic notes, and conversations about the networks themselves. Personal community refers to the people that one is connected with in some other way than only through social media. Thematic notes is the level where people specifically post together about certain subject matters and topics that they keep returning to, regardless whether those topics are centric to the individuals, their location, their interests, religion, or ideologies. And the third level of connection is observed when those smaller personal communities and their thematic notes intersect around a specific topic. When the popular online topics enter offline spaces and conversations, it is a sign of social media activism breaking its limitations and reaching out to 'communities and groups who do not have access to, or the media literacy to engage in, those online discussions', says Kemekenidou (2020, p. 236).

Technology-enabled and/or enhanced activism facilitates several new practices, such as sharing ceremonial behaviour, amplification, informal fellowship (Stewart & Schultze, 2019), consensus mobilisation or persuasive action (Foster, 2019), and 'interconnected engagement repertoires that blend online and offline tactics' (Dennis, 2018, pp. 13–14). Digital activism is also broad-reaching, more immediate, and impactful compared to traditional activism and can be categorised into the spectator, transitional, or gladiatorial activities (George & Leidner, 2019). The activists must understand the opportunities and limitations of digital platforms to be able to utilise them most effectively. Some platforms for live streaming videos are less participatory and interactive than other forms of social media and altogether different from in-person participation; however, live streaming also blends various aspects of human and technology, politics, and journalism and provides unedited insight into the event and actions, dangers, and possibilities of protests (Thornburn, 2015). Jasmine Revolution in Tunisia and the Egyptian revolution of 2011 are great examples of how Facebook, Twitter, and social media played a crucial role in mobilising politically inexperienced but technologically savvy youth (Gerbaudo, 2012). Social media provided activists safe space to connect and assemble while streets and public spaces were heavily monitored and policed; nonetheless, it is important to note that mobilisation was limited due to low levels of connectivity and a low percentage of households having Internet access. Another important aspect for activists to understand is the distinction between reaching critical mass in organising protest events and further consequences. While digital mediums can be used to trigger emotional responses, to mobilise and inform, for true civic engagement to occur, it is imperative to foster 'the empowerment of learners' through organisation, education, agitation, and community building (Ghobadi & Clegg, 2015). It is important to recognise that the Internet can act as both liberation technology that enables creation and actions of new networks and as repressive control technology, when online actions can be subjected to horizontal and vertical surveillance (Greijdanus et al., 2020). The assumption of anonymity can easily be shattered as the Internet can be used to track down the activists (Ghobadi & Clegg, 2015). Discussing the role of Internet, Peter Knapp pointed out that the access to activism online is dependent on one's country's politics, firewalls, Internet access, time zones; however, it allows the span of influence and access to expand, for example, London-based activists can go to the Shell Headquarters whereas a Nigerian activist can go to the Niger delta.

Continuous growth of non-violent resistance may be considered as both a sign of success and one of failure. Chenoweth (2020) believes that information technology and new channels of communications enable people to learn about events and happenings that previously went unreported, and as more segments of society are valuing and expect fair treatment and protection of their rights, people around the world are seeing civil resistance as a legitimate and successful tool for creating the change. However, this also highlights the failing of the governments and institutions to address some rooted prejudices and to prevent new injustices, which creates further demand for civil resistance. As activists and movements discover new avenues and spaces to grow and develop their reach, the governments and elite are also finding new ways to establish some control over new threats to their authority.

References

Blodgett, B. and Tapia, A. (2011) Do avatars dream of electronic picket lines? The blurring of work and play in virtual environments. *Information Technology & People*, 24 (1), pp. 26–45.

Castells, M. (2015) *Networks of outrage and hope: social movements in the Internet age*. Cambridge: Polity Press.

Chenoweth, E. (2020) The future of nonviolent resistance. *Journal of Democracy*, 31 (3), pp. 69–84.

Dearden, L. (2020) British far right "becoming more racist" after Black Lives Matter protests, report finds. *The Independent*. Available from: <www.independent.co.uk/news/uk/home-news/far-right-black-lives-matter-protests-racism-patriotic-alternative-hope-not-hate-a9672401.html> [Accessed 2 September 2023].

Dennis J. (2018) *Beyond slacktivism: political participation on social media*. Palgrave Macmillan.

Foster, M. D. (2019) "Use it or lose it": how online activism moderates the protective properties of gender identity for well-being. *Computers in Human Behaviour*, 96, pp. 163–173.

Fotopoulos, A. (2014) Digital and networked by default? Women's organisations and the social imaginary of networked feminism. *New Media & Society* [Online]. Available from: <http://nms.sagepub.com/content/early/2014/09/29/1461444814552264> [Accessed on 16 March 2021].

George, J.J. and Leidner, D.E. (2019) From clicktivism to hacktivism: understanding digital activism. *Information and Organization*, 29 (3).

Gerbaudo, P. (2012) *Tweets and the streets: Social media and contemporary activism*. London: Pluto Press.

Gerbaudo, P. (2018) Social media and populism: An elective affinity? *Media, Culture & Society*, 40 (5), pp. 745–753.

Ghobadi, S. and Clegg, S. (2015) "These days will never be forgotten . . .": a critical mass approach to online activism. *Information and Organization*, 25, pp. 52–71.

Greijdanus, H., Matos Fernandes, C. A., Turner-Zwinkels, F., Honari, A., Roos, C. A., Rosenbuch, H. and Postmes, T. (2020) The psychology of online activism and social movements: relations between online and offline collective action. *Current Opinion in Psychology*, 35, pp. 49–54.

Heard-Garris, N. (2021) Vicarious racism explained in age of Black Lives Matter. *PsycomPro*. Available from: <https://pro.psycom.net/special_reports/bipoc-mental-health-awareness-racism-in-psychiatry/vicarious-racism-in-age-of-black-lives-matter> [Accessed 2 September 2023].

Jones, R. H. (2005) Sites of engagement as sites of attention: time, space and culture in electronic discourse. In: Norris, S. and Jones, R. H. eds. *Discourse in action: introducing mediated discourse analysis*. Abingdon: Routledge, pp. 141–154.

Kemekenidou, P. (2020) 11 r/ChokeABitch: feminist tactics against hate speech in capitalist social media platforms. In: Polak, S. and Trottier, D. eds. *Violence and trolling on social media: history, affect, and effects of online vitriol*. Amsterdam: Amsterdam University Press, pp. 233–250.

Madison, N. and Klang, M. (2020) The case for digital activism: refuting the fallacies of slacktivism. *Journal of Digital Social Research*, 2 (2), pp. 28–47.

Moynihan, H. (2021) New UK bill can fight fresh wave of online racist abuse. *Chatham House* [Online], 21 July. Available from: <www.chathamhouse.org/2021/07/new-uk-bill-can-fight-fresh-wave-online-racist-abuse> [Accessed 10 October 2023].

Putnam, R. D. (1993) The prosperous community. *The American Prospect* [Online], 4 (13). Available from: <http://faculty.washington.edu/matsueda/courses/590/Readings/Putham%201993%20Am%20Prospect.pdf> [Accessed 12 September 2021].

Shukaitis, S. (2009a) *Imaginal machines: autonomy & self-organization in the revolutions of everyday life*. Brooklyn: Autonomedia.

Shukaitis, S. (2009b) *Combination acts: notes on collective practice in the undercommons*. Brooklyn: Autonomedia.

Stewart, M. and Schultze, U. (2019) Producing solidarity in social media activism: the case of My Stealthy Freedom. *Information and Organization*, 29.

Thornburn, E. D. (2015) Assemblages: live streaming dissent in the "Quebec Spring". In: Trottier, D. and Fuchs, C. eds. *Social media, politics and the state: protests, revolutions, riots, crime and policing in the age of Facebook, Twitter and YouTube*. New York: Routledge, pp. 149–167.

Turan, J.M., Elafros, M.A., Logie, C.H. et al. Challenges and opportunities in examining and addressing intersectional stigma and health. *BMC Med* 17, 7 (2019). Available from: <https://doi.org/10.1186/s12916-018-1246-9>.

van Stekelenburgh, J. and Klandersmans, B. (2013) The social psychology of protest. *Current Sociology Review*, 61 (5–6), pp. 886–905.

4 Articulating events of dissent

4.1 The growth of distrust and disinformation in the digital age

As technological development is accelerating in an unprecedented speed, it is virtually impossible to forecast what the future will bring. A little more than a decade ago, during the Arab Spring of 2010–2012, the protesters used social media to rally their forces and spread their message to the wider world. On the other hand, memes, fake news stories, and Facebook posts were used to spread disinformation and to target the protesters. Since then, two major developments rooted in further advances of artificial intelligence (AI) have changed the playing field: the increase of online disinformation, driven by the fake accounts (bots), deepfake photographs, and videos, and the rise of AI-enabled surveillance (Patheram et al., 2020). 'Disinformation is getting an upgrade', warned American behavioural scientist and expert on disinformation and violent extremism Todd C. Helmus (2022, n.p.). The year 2023 saw a development – ChatGPT was made available and accessible to the majority of Internet users and prompted an outpouring of concern across the world, showing how much further AI has developed than many had expected and exposing how unprepared the governments, markets, and societies are for such a change as they are still grappling to comprehend the upcoming disruption and impact it will have on the future of individuals, industries, and our way of living.

Deepfake videos, voice cloning, generative text, and other AI-generated fake content are becoming more convincing and provide an exceedingly compelling method for channelling disinformation, with various webpages and software packages offering access to deepfake and related services (Helmus, 2022). It is impossible to overestimate the role of the Internet, social media, new technologies, and software packages in enabling and amplifying the exceedingly intrusive public-opinion-forming campaigns that now have a worldwide reach. Some researchers suggest that within the next five years, approximately 90% of online content will be artificially generated (Patheram et al., 2020). Deepfake images, videos, voice-cloning recordings, and generative text have all been widely reported to have been used to spread disinformation during

DOI: 10.4324/9781003460640-5

major campaigns and critical events, such as the US president election campaigns, Russia's war in Ukraine, and Kremlin's attempts to discredit European governments. Drawing on studies on the influence of Russia in the US and European elections, Rogers and Niederer (2020) observe a shift in Russia's disinformation campaigning 'from inflaming conflict with the West to stirring it within the West' (p. 20), where such campaigning not only seeks to create the narratives that divide but 'also employs computational means to inflate and amplify them through bot work, fake following, astroturfing, the creation of front groups and other artificial publicity tactics' (Ibid. p. 20). China is suspected to have used mass-produced fake news stories in a *barrage jamming* technique in an attempt to overwhelm the hashtag #Xinjiang and make the readers see tweets depicting cotton fields of Xinjiang as opposed to the tweets about human rights abuses in the forced labour camps (Helmus, 2022). The growing possibility of fake content also enables governments and institutions to dismiss genuine footage and content as being false – 'in a world where anything can be faked, everything can be denied' (Patheram et al., 2020, n.p.). For example in 2020, a Republican candidate running for Congress proposed that the video of George Floyd's murder was created using deepfake technology (Spocchia, 2020).

In the UK, trust in the media remains one of the lowest among the 28 countries surveyed in the 2022 annual Edelman Trust Barometer, in which 32,000 people took part. Reportedly, only 37% of 1,150 people surveyed in the UK said they trusted the media – the only two countries where people were less trusting of the news industry were Japan and South Korea (Majid, 2023). The same report shows that journalists are among the least-trusted institutional leaders – only 47% of respondents said they trusted journalists, and only government leaders scored worse, at 41%. In contrast, people thought search engines to be most reliable among the news sources, trusted by 63% of the respondents, while 59% trusted traditional media, and 41% claimed to trust social media making it the least trusted but still significant news source. Majid (2023, n.p.) cites Richard Edelman expressing concern that the cost-of-living crisis, the war in Ukraine, inflation, food insecurity, a continuing loss of belief in media, and the rise of disinformation following the COVID-19 pandemic contributed to a 'descent from distrust to acute polarisation in society'. There is also a growing concern among the scholars about how new technological developments will alter democracies and people's shared realities across the globe.

4.2 Development of propaganda model and its relevance in a changing world

4.2.1 *Propaganda model*

In 1988, Herman and Chomsky proposed their 'propaganda model' to explain the invisible pulls and the power concentrations which modify our thoughts and habits. The model posed that the mass media serves the interests of the wealthy and powerful, sifting the 'raw material of news' through five 'filters' of ownership, income, funding, flak, and national control mechanisms. In their book *Manufacturing Consent* (1988), Herman and Chomsky defined those filters as:

> (1) the size, concentrated ownership, owner wealth, and profit orientation of the dominant mass-media firms; (2) advertising as the primary income source of the mass media; (3) the reliance of the media on information provided by government, business, and 'experts' funded and approved by these primary sources and agents of power; (4) 'flak' as a means of disciplining the media; and (5) 'anticommunism' as a national religion and control mechanism. . . . They fix the premises of discourse and interpretation, and the definition of what is newsworthy in the first place, and they explain the basis and operations of what amounts to propaganda campaigns.
>
> (p. 2)

Although a lot has changed in the world since the *propaganda model* was introduced, the same processes remain at work, and so 30 years later, Broudy and Tanji (2018, p. 100) wrote: 'Safeguarding today's System demands both the routine maintenance of compliant actors working within as well as accommodating media without, which can effectively educate the masses by reflecting the policies of established power'. Although some authors effectively demonstrate how fluidly Herman and Chomsky's proposed model can be adapted to the changing times and changing strategies of control (Cooley, 2010), others indicate some weaknesses. For example Fuchs (2018) opposes the lack of the systematic theory of society and capitalism in Herman and Chomsky's writings and notes the absence of clear definitions of the roles of culture, ideology, and propaganda. Alongside the analysis of the five filters and their application to the Internet and digital media, Fuchs notes that it is unclear why there are five elements to the model and how they were theoretically justified. He also queries the omission of 'entertainment and the spectacle as a filter that displaces and colonises political communication' (Fuchs, 2018, p. 72). Freedman (2017) tests the effectiveness of the model using a curious example of the British tabloid newspaper the *Daily Mirror*, which dropped its usual celebrity scandal stories and launched a petition that opposed the proposed war on Iraq in January 2003 – a petition that was signed by over 220,000 people. Herman and Chomsky themselves acknowledge that 'the mass media are not a monolith on all issues. Where the powerful are in disagreement, there will be a certain diversity of tactical judgements on how to attain generally shared aims, reflected in media debate' (Herman & Chomsky, 1988a, np). Freedman (2017) therefore positions this as the premise of his main criticism of the propaganda model – it is not that the model does not admit there would be exceptions and scope for dissent within the corporate media but rather that there is very little focus and no examples of such exceptions; therefore, the propaganda model 'finds it difficult to offer a fully worked-out picture of consensus and conflict' (p. 62). Using the examples of the Mirror's petition and their articles against the war in Iraq, Freedman suggests that the moments of crisis create meaningful possibilities for transformative action:

> [T]imes at which established structures start to wobble, when previously hidden tensions emerge and when new actors are called for, abnormal circumstances are crucial in alerting us to the possibilities of both new kinds of political action and new kinds of media coverage.
>
> (Freedman, 2017, p. 62)

Over the years, academic researchers have identified several methods frequently used to manipulate the news. Some mainstream media sources, particularly those specialising in 'soft' news, use priority distortion in viewers' (or readers') minds by reporting on some celebrity drama, which is followed by a story relating to political or social welfare issues, which 'immobilizes them in the face of such absurd contrasts and further devalues any reasonable interest in political engagement' (Cooley, 2010, p. 591). In conversation about the XR's Free the Press action, which was aimed at making the public aware of who owns UK's media and controls the news, XR activist Jon Fuller also noted that the right-wing media will occasionally publish articles stating that the scientists are concerned about the climate emergency but will not explain the details, making such news complex to understand to their readers. This is consistent with Habermas, who argues that 'reporting facts as human-interest stories, mixing information with entertainment, arranging material episodically, and breaking down complex relationships into smaller fragments – all of this comes together to form a syndrome that works to depoliticize public communication' (Habermas, 1998, paraphrased in Fuchs, 2018, p. 72). Coverage of important social issues can also be easily distorted and controlled by misinformation and omission while 'the public and mid-level policymakers are basing their decisions on such filtered information' (Cooley, 2010, p. 592).

Perspectivism is a concept that essentially refers to the way we interpret the world around us based on our views and perceptions, and it is a result of the impact that ideology and material conditions have on news reporting, which in itself is a process of taking 'the raw materials of selected events' and carving them into narratives (Goss, 2015). The narratives that news media produce by shaping and interpreting events through the reporter's (or the news outlet owner's) ideological lens often create a dichotomy between two pre-existing opposing positions of 'us' and 'them'. To create such binary, 'they' are positioned as a problematic, disruptive group of outsiders, sometimes extreme, violent, and dangerous, whose actions, intents, and nature are always transparent to 'us', whereas 'they' can never fully understand the complexity of virtuous 'us' (Goss, 2015, p. 244). For example Edward Snowden's stories posed a danger to established systems, and so the power structures used the media to immediately discredit his character by describing him as a 'traitor', 'criminal', and 'thief' – a campaign that was reinforced by the pervasive societal ignorance, which is often a sign of hegemonic dominations (Broudy & Tanji, 2018). Earlier discussed right-wing media's reaction to the XR's blockade of Murdoch's printworks presented another example of an attempt to discredit the movement, as right-wing press used character assassination as a trusted tool to deal with a threat to the establishment. Miller and Ko's (2012) analysis of media narratives during the Iraq conflict found that the majority of the references cited by four major news outlets came from either Iraqi or American government or military officials, which supports Herman and Chomsky's claim that official sources can shape the narratives presented in the mainstream media. Frequently, the ruling elite will manipulate the concepts of national security and intelligence to control any information leaks that could pose danger to the ruling classes and corporations by defining those who question the corporate, political, and military powers as traitors: 'In the times when the interests of the corporate and political elite have merged . . . mass media have had a direct hand in painting unflattering portraits of figures who call public attention to abuses' (Broudy & Tanji, 2018, p. 102). Mainstream media can also be used to drive the general public away from the political debates by conditioning people to support the policies of political elites' that are claimed to be essential for state security and public safety but in effect are aimed at silencing so called 'security leaks' and voices that could be potentially dangerous for the ruling elite. Broudy and Tanji (2018, p. 94) suggest that 'state security' should be read as 'system security' as it is aimed to protect the global capitalist system through digital media control mechanisms and propose this filter as a component of the Propaganda Model's conceptual framework.

'Buying out' of journalists or publications by intelligence and related organisations has been proposed as a sixth filter to the propaganda model, as Boyd-Barrett (2004) observed that while the evidence of the operation of some of the filters in their research was weaker, the framework of media propaganda analysis based on Herman and Chomsky's model was still strong and relevant. The propaganda model does not assume that individual journalists purposefully make routine decisions to align themselves with the interests of those in power; however, the constraints and meanings for the shaping of the narrative are built into the system in such a way that they are understood as common sense (Klaehn, 2003). This view is supported by Steve Tooze, a former tabloid journalist who joined XR and was present at the action at Broxbourne, and Zoë Blackler, a journalist and radio producer, who discussed their experiences on Peter Knapp's 'Tipping Points' podcast (Knapp, 2022). Both journalists shared their experiences of the internal workings of the tabloids and newspapers, admitting that reporters are not exactly free to cover the topics they feel are important (e.g. the climate emergency), as the power structures within their corporations make it very clear what stories and narratives are acceptable. Sometimes, publishing the coverage of events, such as protests, may be the only avenue to touch on the issues that lie at the heart of the event or the movement; however, for a journalist to be able to cover the event, it would have to be significant in its scope or the disruption caused, and in such a way the media may act as a catalyst for more and more disruptive protest events.

Denouncement of the protest, as well as the whole movement, was evident in the media's coverage of the Broxbourne printworks blockade. The journalists may create scandalous headlines and narratives by depicting the activists as members of a cult, questioning their common sense, and focusing on demeaning portrayals. In such way, the readers' emotion and understanding of democracy can be manipulated in an attempt to bury the concerns and true purpose behind the action and to fuel public frustration. This, however, often paints the wrong picture, claims Peter Knapp from Extinction Rebellion. He firmly believes that there is a significant difference between public's support to the movement's actions and public's support of the cause. He says that the statement 'your actions are harming your cause' is usually made assuming that the movement's cause is to get the public supporting the activist group, but the actual cause (in Extinction Rebellion's case) is getting more pressure to get the government to take climate action. Peter believes that this is something that people struggle to comprehend, wondering why would the public be supportive of the climate action if they don't support the activist groups. Peter's response to this question is that some people initially learn about the climate emergency and the lack of government action through the disruption, which also allows the space for the journalists to report on it because otherwise it isn't news. Jon Fuller, another Extinction Rebellion activist we spoke with, said that a lot of Extinction Rebellion activists adapt the attitude that they don't know where the public tipping point is when it comes to disruptive events, so they need to try everything. Most in Extinction Rebellion objected to the Canning Town public transport action and didn't want it repeated. However, those who supported more dynamic forms of protest, which did cause public disruption, set up Insulate Britain and (later) Just Stop Oil. Just Stop Oil now organises more public disruptive events, while Extinction Rebellion focus their actions against the fossil fuel corporations and their influences in the government and media. Many will see Extinction Rebellion as more of a 'safe half way house' now, not as radical as Just Stop Oil or Insulate Britain.

4.2.2   *Propaganda, the Internet, and the cycle of co-dependency*

As information communication technologies continue to evolve and change the ways in which individuals engage in the public information domain, new ways of influencing, new tactics and means of spreading propaganda, and adapting propaganda messages have also emerged, providing new forms of data that can be used to complement traditional forms (Broniecki & Hanchar, 2017). Groups and businesses use bots to post fake comments or reviews to manipulate algorithms to either promote disinformation or create a cognitive bias, and something trending online can often lead to media coverage, which provides gateways to staging events or scandals to gain media interest (Wanless, 2017; Roese, 2018). Wanless proposes the concept of participatory propaganda model, which specifically concentrates on propaganda campaigns that are run through the use of online communities, where

> propaganda moves beyond a traditional, unidirectional 'one-to-many' form of communication, to a 'one-to-many-to-many more' form where each 'target' of influence (an individual or group which is the object of persuasion) can in theory become the new 'originator' (subject) of content production and distribution, spreading persuasive messaging to others in a 'snowball' effect.
>
> (Wanless, 2017, p. 6)

Some may still believe that social media and the Internet generally foster democratic communications and a participatory culture, somehow overcoming the power hierarchies and creating a level and honest playing field. However, it is worth remembering that the dominant social media platforms have concentrated ownership and form a very concentrated market. Google has the monopoly of 71% of the worldwide searches, and Facebook and WhatsApp, which it owns, account for 48% of world's users of the top social media platforms (Fuchs, 2018). Entertainment-focused content and spectacles have always attracted more advertising. While on television and in the printed press, the advertisers are targeting specific audiences, on social media, multiple audiences can be targeted at once. Facebook and Twitter (now called X) users can pay to promote postings, Twitter and Google allow targeted ads, and Twitter also enables the promotion of trends, all of which allow for the advertising to work as a filter in several ways. Large corporations with very substantial advertising budgets are able to confront large, targeted audiences, while regular content may become ever more difficult to discern from advertising, allowing the corporations to deceive users and act almost like news media (Fuchs, 2018). Viral marketers understand that the majority of social media users are more susceptible to and more supportive of the posts and information shared by what they believe to be an authentic user 'next door', and so in some cases viral marketing companies will 'hide' the product behind the message they plant on the social media, hoping for the natural amplification to occur when other users will start sharing the post and create a new 'media hype' (Roese, 2018). The problem with all this, explains Taylor (2021), is that the Internet was meant to democratise, enable, and engage people in the public sphere; however, this medium that was supposed to give power to the people now has a business model in not informing the public but selling as many ads as possible for profit. 'We've ceded power of the primary space people "come together to freely discuss and identify societal problems" to a business model that prioritises profit above all else, with no democratic accountability' (Taylor, 2021, p. 88). However, it is also important to remember that the Internet and social media facilitate positive communications, too. Peter Knapp from Extinction Rebellion acknowledges that although the social media is controlled by the billionaires in the same way as the press, it is, he believes, incredibly fragile. He agrees it remains incredibly important as Twitter (X) and other social platforms have been incredibly powerful in reporting what the news media don't report and filling in the gaps of what other forms of media do not.

The Internet and mass self-communication brought a new phenomenon of user-generated content, which, contrary to popular belief, does not imply political diversity but shifts the question about communication power from the control of production, in traditional broadcasting and publishing, to the control of attention and visibility (Fuchs, 2018). This interconnectivity has also enhanced the interdependence among news media, social media, and the users where the users depend on social media as part of their everyday lives and as sources of information. They also depend on news media to deliver verified facts. However, if news media is no longer relied upon to report the news, in such cases news media will pick up social media topics to investigate, validate, and present as part of the 'hype cycle' (Roese, 2018, p. 328). This brings the focus back to the dominant online news providers, and their spending power, which enables a boost to online attention through buying likes, followers, and re-posts and reputational inequalities which grant small, elite groups to dominate online visibility and automated accounts (bots) which, while appearing human-like, are used to distort attention, terrorise, and harass users. It is important to remember that bots are owned, controlled, and programmed by people, so while 'the political bot does not have political attitudes, morals and interests, its behaviour is shaped by human beings who have particular political interests' (Fuchs, 2018, p. 80). 'In the digital age, lobbying for certain interests has been extended to social media and . . . now aims to directly transmit political messages to as many users as possible' (Ibid, p. 81). Bradshaw (2020) notes that bots are programmed to post, share, and engage with users online, and they are able to post much more frequently than humans, thus by sharing, liking, re-posting, or posting comments, those automated accounts can create an almost instant trend, an artificially created sense of importance, momentum, or popularity around a particular idea, person, or event. Not only that but also bots can be a very powerful tool used to target and harass journalists, activists, and others, flooding them with threats and hate comments from artificially created accounts. Sock puppets, as described by Rogers and Niederer (2020), are also part of the collection of actors and software used for online propaganda, as they assume the false identity of grassroots organiser or a concerned individual to create and circulate political content, organise events, and mobilise audiences. Another closely related term for deceitful content is astroturfing. It is essentially a masked political content, an 'artificial seeding of newspapers and other content providers with political (or corporate) advertising disguised as genuine citizen concerns' (Ibid, p. 25).

Each of our interactions with technology leaves behind an immense amount of data which can be aggregated and used to create detailed pictures of who we are, not only as consumers but also as citizens and voters, making us oblivious targets of not only marketing but also political and propaganda campaigns (Bradshaw, 2020). Most Internet search engines and social media sites use algorithms that ultimately hide opposing or varying information and only provide users with content that is based on their previous searches or online interactions, thus manipulating users' feed and providing echo chambers that evolve further by sharing messages, using influencers to share or promote content, and endorsing ideas and political views (Wanless, 2017; Broniecki & Hanchar, 2017). Facebook and Google algorithms are kept as corporate secrets, and the combination of centralised ownership of those companies and the platforms being important news sources results in the fact that 'ownership also means control over algorithms that determine news sources for a significant part of the population' (Fuchs, 2018, p. 73). That 'selective exposure' and audience fragmentation, presented by social media, can be seen as a threat to democracy itself, argues Dennis (2019, p. 126). Taylor (2021) outright calls YouTube 'a hot-bed of radicalisation', explaining how, since being purchased by Google and now enabling Google to track and record its users' behaviour, YouTube has come to serve another purpose, and 'through combination of monetisation and personalisation has been a boon for radical and fringe ideologies, particularly on the far-right' (Taylor, 2021, pp. 65–67). Fuchs (2018, p. 83) agrees that in the current political climate, 'fascism and right-wing extremism on social media are to a significant degree public forms of communication' and 'social media is certainly a right-wing attack machine'(ibid, p. 83). A study which analysed half a million tweets in the month before 2017 Dutch general election showed 'a notable asymmetry in the distribution of targets of troll-like behaviour and sock puppetry across the political spectrum, where left-wing politicians are most often targeted by negative mentions, while right-wing politicians receive support' (Rogers & Niederer, 2020, p. 36). More worryingly, the troll content was found to be cited by some reputable news sources at least 30 times, and among the cited accounts were a number of fake news organisations, fake political parties accounts, and fake concerned citizens.

Rogers and Niederer (2020, pp. 25–26) identify 'dark posts' and 'image macros' as popular formats that are used by political operatives to attract the publics to divisive content online. 'Dark posts', also known as promoted posts on Facebook, refer to micro-targeted ads that employ algorithms to assemble 'keyword publics' by querying the Facebook advertising platforms for certain words or word combinations and then sending targeted political content or advertising to the news feeds of people who have such interests. 'Image macros', commonly referred to as 'memes', are also a popular format for political messaging and have been proven to be among the most engaged with and most shared content on the platform. Prier (2017) explains the model:

> One of the primary principles of propaganda is that the message must resonate with the target. Therefore, when presented with information that is within your belief structure, your bias is confirmed and you accept the propaganda. If it is outside of your network, you may initially reject the story, but the volume of information may create an availability heuristic in your mind. Over time, the propaganda becomes normalised – and even believable. It is confirmed when a fake news story is reported by the mainstream media, which has become reliant on social media for spreading and receiving news.

This chapter demonstrates that although the propaganda model is still relevant in today's conversations about social movements and protests, the model needs to be extended and adapted to reflect the workings of the digital platforms and technological developments. A lot of the issues discussed in this chapter are not necessarily specific to propaganda but to power systems in general. Despite digital capitalism, the Internet and social media are social systems, so to analyse them, we must consider the interactions and significance of economy, culture, politics, processes, objects, and subjects (Fuchs, 2018). And even though the accessibility and widespread use of the Internet have led to 'some of the most tribal and primitive acts in our history, alongside some of the most utopian and military advanced' (Kozinets, 2015, p. 13), social media and society are not exclusively ruled by the right wing. Studies show that 'left-wing activists can challenge ideology by characterising those attacked in positive terms, using satire, humour, sarcasm, provide links and arguments showing the world's complexity and contradictions, argumentative dialectical reversals' (Fuchs, 2018). Our conversations with Jamie Klingler, Jon Fuller, and Peter Knapp also demonstrated how social media can be, and has very recently been, used to accelerate and amplify the voices of dissent and call society to action. A change to any given sphere is likely to cause paradigms to shift in other fields, whether it is a private or a public sphere, and over the past couple of decades, we have witnessed how technological changes have infiltrated other areas of life and technology, and the digital platforms have become important actors in their own right. The race to embrace and harness the potential of any new inventions is a never-ending one, and it continues to drive the developments further. However, not all changes can be forecasted or planned for, and when they happen, some social actors demonstrate their ability to adapt, while others rush to mobilise and establish stricter forms of control.

References

Boyd-Barrett, O. (2004) Judith Miller, The New York Times, and the Propaganda Model. *Journalism Studies*, 5 (4), pp. 435–449.

Bradshaw, S. (2020) Influence Operations and Disinformation of Social Media. *Modern Conflict and Artificial Intelligence Report. Centre for international Governance Innovation*, pp. 41–47. Available from: <www.jstor.org/stable/resrep27510.9;.

Broniecki, P. and Hanchar, A. (2017) Data Innovation for International Development: An Overview of Natural Language Processing for Qualitative Data Analysis. In: *Proceedings of the 2017 International Conference on the Frontiers and Advances in Data Science (FADS)*, 23–25 October. Xian: IEEE.

Broudy, D. and Tanji, M. (2018) System Security: A Missing Filter for the Propaganda Model? In: Pedro-Cerañana, J., Broudy, D. and Klaehn, J. eds. *The Propaganda Model Today: Filtering Perception and Awareness*. London: University of Westminster Press, pp. 93–106.

Cooley, A. (2010) Failed States in Education: Chomsky on Dissent, Propaganda, and Reclaiming Democracy in the Media Spectacle. *Educational Studies*, 46, pp. 579–605.

Dennis J. (2019) *Beyond Slacktivism: Political Participation on Social Media*. New York: Palgrave Macmillan.

Freedman, D. (2017) 'Smooth Operator?' The Propaganda Model and Moments of Crisis. *Westminster Papers in Communication and Culture*, 6 (2), pp. 59–72. Available from: <https://doi.org/10.16997/wpcc.124>.

Fuchs, C. (2018) Propaganda 2.0: Herman and Chomsky's Propaganda Model in the Age of the Internet, Big Data and Social Media. In: Pedro-Cerañana, J., Broudy, D. and Klaehn, J. eds. *The Propaganda Model Today: Filtering Perception and Awareness*. London: University of Westminster Press, pp. 71–92.

Goss, B.M. (2015) The World Is Not Enough. *Journalism Studies*, 16 (2), pp. 243–258.

Habermas, J. (1998) *Between Facts and Norms: Contributions to a Discourse Theory of Law and Democracy*. Cambridge, MA: The MIT Press, p. 377 [Quoted in: Fuchs, C. (2018) Propaganda 2.0: Herman and Chomsky's Propaganda Model in the Age of the Internet, Big Data and Social Media. In: Pedro-Cerañana, J., Broudy, D. and Klaehn, J. eds. The Propaganda Model Today: Filtering Perception and Awareness. London: University of Westminster Press, pp. 71–92].

Helmus, T.C. (2022) *Artificial Intelligence, Deepfakes, and Disinformation: A Primer* [Online]. Santa Monica: RAND Corporation. Available from: <www.rand.org/pubs/perspectives/PEA1043-1.html> [Accessed 12 August 2023].

Herman, E.S. and Chomsky, N. (1988) *Manufacturing Consent: The Political Economy of the Mass Media*. New York: Pantheon Books.

Klaehn, J. (2003) Behind the Invisible Curtain of Scholarly Criticism: Revisiting the Propaganda Model. *Journalism Studies*, 4 (3), pp. 359–369.

Knapp, P. (2022) #16 Zoë Blackler and Steve Tooze on the Power of the Media, and Its Responsibility to Cover the Climate Crisis. *Tipping Points*, Spotify [Podcast], 4 March. Available from: <https://open.spotify.com/episode/1bDSLKIpNiRfa6K8O0h97y> [Accessed 5 August 2023].

Kozinets, R.V. (2015) *Netnography: Redefined.* Thousand Oaks: SAGE.

Majid, A. (2023) Trust in Media up in UK But Remains among Lowest in the World, Edelman Survey Finds. *Press Gazette* [Online], 18 January. Available from: <https://pressgazette.co.uk/media-audience-and-business-data/trust-media-increase-uk-us-edelman/> [Accessed 13 August 2023].

Miller, N.W. and Ko, R.S. (2012) Constructing Narratives as a Means of Legitimizing Political Power: Contextualizing the Propaganda Model in Iraq. *International Journal of Contemporary Iraqi Studies*, 6 (1), pp. 97–116.

Patheram, A., Shearer, E., Stirling, R. and Westgarth, T. (2020) *Fakes, Flies and Facial Recognition. Artificial Intelligence and the New Worlds of Protest., Revolution and Digital Interventionism* [Online]. Oxford: Oxford Insights. Available from: <www.oxfordinsights.com/artificial-intelligence-revolution-and-digital-interventionism> [Accessed 10 August 2023].

Prier, J. (2017) Commanding the Trend: Social Media as Information Warfare. *Strategic Studies Quarterly*, 11 (4), 50–85. www.jstor.org/stable/26271634.

Roese, V. (2018) You Won't Believe How Codependent They Are Or: Media Hype and the Interaction of News Media, Social Media and the User. In: Pedro-Cerañana, J., Broudy, D. and Klaehn, J. eds. *The Propaganda Model Today: Filtering Perception and Awareness*. London: University of Westminster Press, pp. 313–332.

Rogers, R. and Niederer, S. (2020) *The Politics of Social Media Manipulation*. Amsterdam: Amsterdam University Press.

Spocchia, G. (2020) Republican Candidate Shares Conspiracy Theory That George Floyd Murder Was Faked. *The Independent*. Available from: <www.independent.co.uk/news/world/americas/us-politics/george-floyd-murder-fake-conspiracy-theory-hoax-republican-gop-missouri-a9580896.htm> [Accessed 10 August 2023].

Taylor, K. (2021) *The Little Black Book of Data and Democracy*. London: Byline Times.

Wanless, A. (2017) A Participatory Propaganda Model. *Social Media & Social Order, Culture Conflict 2.0* [Online]. Available from: <www.academia.edu/37951615/A_Participatory_Propaganda_Model_SM_pdf> [Accessed 7 June 2021].

5　The eventalisation of the political

5.1　Interpreting and framing of the social sphere

Researchers and theorists who work within the context of an interpretivist paradigm will often adopt a subjectivist approach to their analysis of the social world. An interpretivist paradigm is informed by an endeavour to understand the fundamental nature of the social world at the level of subjective experience (Burrell & Morgan, 1979). Subjectivism views social phenomena as 'created through the perceptions and consequent actions of affected social actors' (Saunders et al., 2012, p. 131). Social constructionism approaches reality as constructed by social actors and their perceptions and interpretations of reality, allowing such perceptions to affect the social interactions between those actors. Bruno Latour's (2005) actor–network theory suggests a similar approach proposing that the social world emerges from a constantly changing network of associations and relationships and is made of interactions among people, ideas, objects, events, and processes. As social movements organise protest events in response to the changing conditions in the world, to understand the motives and intentions of the participants and activists it is important to first get to know their subjective reality. Public engagement and reactions can often be vital for the success of the event and the cause of the movement itself as they can drive or hinder the social change, therefore understanding how public opinions and knowledge are created and manipulated by the traditional and social media sources is also crucial.

Abderrahim and Gutiérrez-Colón Plana (2021, p. 39) use social constructivism theory in cognitive development research to demonstrate that an individual cannot acquire what they don't know independently; they require guidance and a facilitator with a more advanced cognitive development to create a collaborative experiential learning experience. In a society based on ever-increasing flows of information, human capacity to perceive, process, and decode the symbolic languages plays a vital role, and 'the possibility of exerting power shifts from the contents of communication and societal exchanges to the formal structures, to the codes that organise the flow of information' (Melucci, 1995, p. 135). In this age of increased information flow, individuals

DOI: 10.4324/9781003460640-6

and groups have to construct their lives and identities, faced with the growing intervention and control into spheres that used to be considered private or subjective (i.e. one's sexuality, relations, emotional processes, motives, and desires). Here, agencies form and control the information and communications and determine policies and brandish their power, but these are also the spheres where the individuals and groups can claim their autonomy, realise their search for identity, and self-realise and construct the meaning of what they are and what they do. Those processes generate new forms of power and new forms of opposition, as actors wrestle for control and 'the allocation of socially produced potential for action' (Melucci, 1995, p. 135). The importance of this lies in the understanding that it isn't just individuals undergoing those processes, they also impact whole societies and movements, reminding that we can work more on the processes rather than contents to better face the challenges and complexities of the world (Ibid, p. 141). Understanding how and why stories and narratives are created and applied to inform, manipulate, and change opinions and impact societal change should be the basic and also ultimately important tool in the hands of any social movement, and therefore it was an important topic for this book.

Social scientific theories can be constructed using cultural models (Snodgrass et al., 2020) that assimilate various themes and groups of themes and represent socially transmitted knowledge that is used by members of social groups or cultures to understand relationships among people, things, and processes. According to the anthropologist Morris Opler, cultural systems are made of groups of interrelated themes, and theme identification is a key step in analysing cultures because themes are 'a limited number of dynamic affirmations . . . which control behaviour or stimulate activity' (Opler, 1945, cited in Ryan & Bernard, 2003, p. 2). In the present day, social scientists use a variety of terms to discuss the linkage between themes and how they are expressed – they speak of 'codes', 'categories', 'labels', 'thematic units', 'data bits', and 'concepts' (Ryan & Bernard, 2003). Ryan and Bernard (Ibid) consider themes to be conceptual constructs that link expressions found in texts, images, objects, and sounds. Sentiment analysis is a specific technique based on identifying keywords in the vocabularies associated with and used to express positive and negative emotions (Broniecki & Hanchar, 2017). Although pre-existing understanding of protests as a controversial topic suggested that the events in question would have been the main topic in the newspaper articles covering Sarah Everard vigil, Black Lives Matter UK protests, and the blockade of Broxbourne printworks, recurring themes suggested that the articles were used to support or form opinions on the event driving issues instead. In the case of the media coverage of Sarah Everard vigil, both left- and right-leaning newspapers supported the event; however, a frequent repetition of sentiment-identifying keywords such as 'fear', 'anger', and 'emotions' was observed in the right-leaning newspapers, ultimately resulting in the depiction of crime and violence against women as an emotional issue and informing further discourse analysis which revealed different approaches to the problem by the left-leaning and right-leaning newspapers. An analysis of the language used in the newspaper coverage of the Extinction Rebellion event also revealed several themes: the right-leaning newspapers sought to discredit the movement in several ways, by using demeaning words to describe the activists, by promoting the idea that the movement should be considered a criminal organisation whose actions are aimed to prevent the free speech and thus democracy, and by using interviews with some former members of the movement to highlight the internal conflicts and lack of clear organisation and unity within Extinction Rebellion. Interestingly enough, same papers allowed for a very narrow definition of Extinction Rebellion aims – the question was raised as to why a climate-focused movement would want to question capitalism, discouraging the readers from making any cognitive links between the two. Another theme that emerged through the comparison of the language and argumentation used in left-wing newspapers and right-wing newspapers was the difference in understanding democracy and freedom of speech. Left-leaning newspapers supported protests as a necessary tool for democracy, while right-leaning newspapers accused protesters of preventing the freedom of expression and therefore acting against democracy.

These findings can be used not only to reinforce the Herman and Chomsky (1988) *propaganda model* but also to suggest the possibility of reverse action, as activists can use the same tools and media to position problems and arguments in a particular light and to structure future arguments and events using pre-existing knowledge and understanding of media-framing tendencies.

5.2 The impacts of COVID-19

The change in the way parties and coalitions operate in many countries has created a new dynamic in the way democracy is led, which has given rise to a greater emphasis on the image and campaigns of politicians. The truth and finding resolutions to ongoing issues seem to have been pushed further down the priorities' list, adding more unease and uncertainty in societies that are already dealing with cycles of change through different governments and their complex and continually changing messages (Jarman, 2021). COVID-19 pandemic brought further unexpected changes and created a new unprecedented environment with an increased public focus on the direct impact that the political decisions have on everyday lives. Along with the new restrictions, a change to the 'normal' resulted in social movements and activists finding innovative ways to adapt to the lockdown restrictions. Some took to the streets with socially distanced dissent where people wore masks and stood on designated marks six feet apart while protesting in Jerusalem, women in Warsaw used their cars to block the roads as they protested legislation around abortion laws, and protesters in Lebanon used their vehicles, honking the horns and waving the flags out of the windows. There was also a shift to the digital: artists in Chile created virtual murals on social media depicting anti-government messages, and activists in Hong-Kong spread pro-democracy messages through video games (Pinckney & Rivers, 2020).

Employing diverse tactics makes the movement not only more engaging and accessible but also less vulnerable to repression where the governments may use certain operating environments or conditions as a pretext to restrict and punish dissent. Drawing on Alberto Melucci and Alain Touraine's ideas, Gerbaudo (2020) proposes that social movements embody the spirit of the times, and 'because of their informal nature, they are often the first site in which society's emerging problems are aired' (Ibid, p. 64). Research of Pinckney and Rivers (2020) into how COVID-19 pandemic may have affected the dynamics of individuals' participation in protests proposed micro-foundational dynamics highly likely to have been impacted by the worldwide pandemic. The direct risk of infection while gathering in large groups may have altered someone's decision to participate, and may have had an impact on the 'biographical availability', where during a pandemic activists may lose employment or other opportunities due to lockdown policies, or be affected by a change to their family responsibilities. Additionally, COVID-19 pandemic caused a disruption to normal routines and created a sense 'that we live amid a state of exception, in which normal rules, expectations, and social routines are altered' (Gerbaudo, 2020, p. 62), which may have impacted people's psychological inclination to participate in activism, 'opening psychological space to the possibilities for more radical collective action' (Pinckney & Rivers, 2020, p. 25).

Jarman's (2021, p. 101) analysis of the issues of policing in the COVID-19 pandemic found that the weight placed on scientific advice fluctuated depending on the political goals being pursued, which had a significant impact on policing, 'especially where the politicisation of the police has been driven under the narrative of increasing public scrutiny'. We saw expectations placed on how the police work and what they focus on change, and where the police were expected to follow the political lead to fit in with the needs of political leaders. Public, media, and politicians' reactions to how the police addressed three protest events discussed in earlier chapters reveal the inconsistent expectations, resulting in the police being criticised for being too robust and at the same time too soft, too keen to issue penalties, and, when they tried to engage with people or focused on de-escalation, not holding the line. Where the police chose not to intervene in order to enforce the law and to avert violence, the media was keen to propose the narrative of weak police leadership.

5.3   Policing the 'good' and 'bad' dissent

Assembling into crowds gives people power, and allows them to challenge forms of social control. For those accustomed to holding the whip hand, there is nothing more terrifying than that.

(Reicher, 2022)

Many of the controversial changes to the Police and Crime Bill in 2022 were a direct response to the Extinction Rebellion and Black Lives Matter protests and were brought in to enable the police to put more conditions on static protests, impose start and finish times, set noise limits, and even apply those rules to a demonstration by just one person. The Bill also allows the police to stop and search anyone in the vicinity of a protest. Failure to follow restrictions that the protesters 'knows or ought to have known', even if they have not received a direct order from an officer, is also deemed a crime. A person refusing to follow police directions about how they should protest can be fined up to £2,500, whereas a damage to memorials could lead to up to 10 years in prison. Despite the harsh criticism by the Amnesty International UK, Parliament's Joint Committee on Human Rights, various campaign groups, and even the Shadow Home Secretary, the Home Office has insisted that the Bill respects human rights and does not grant the police, local authorities, or any other body powers to ban protests (BBC, 2022).

Although the Bill received a lot of criticism, it by no means signifies the end of dissent. In conversation, Jon from Extinction Rebellion acknowledged some ground for concern that with the new Policing Bill, there could be a rise in unaccountable action. If before someone was risking a month in prison and now they are risking a potential penalty of several years in prison, this may increase a person's will to make it 'worth it' and proceed with more extreme action. However, it is more likely to depend and be reflective of the inclinations of an individual rather that any movement. Peter Knapp, from Scientists for Extinction Rebellion, does not believe that the increasing level of punishment would have a significant impact. The Bill may dissuade some activists but won't dissuade enough. Pete believes that regardless of the level of penalty, if the cause that brought the dissent is not dealt with, then the protests won't stop happening. It is naïve for the government to think that more police would stop the crime. The only deterrent would be the elimination of the reason why people feel they need to protest; however, politicians who put forward legislation to increase police powers and punishment are insecure and have no empathy, not realising they are setting up the system for failure.

> [T]he drive from politicians to get closer to police, to use the power of the police to underline their popularist and political agendas, and the immensely challenging role officers perform have identified a series of fault lines in society.
>
> (Jarman, 2021, p. 112)

Bleiker (2008, p. 36) proposes that if we push the understanding of democracy beyond an institutionalised framework of procedures, dissenting protests could be viewed as a new kind of democratic participation that makes a meaningful contribution to the theory and practice of global democracy. It is unlikely that in a presence of oppressive political environment, long-needed changes would come from internal institutionalised reforms but rather from sometimes experimental, persistent, externally induced politics of disturbance (Bleiker, 2008).

> Instead of trying to design the institutions which, through supposedly 'impartial' procedures, would reconcile all conflicting interests and values, the task for democratic theorists and politicians should be to envisage the creation of a vibrant 'agonistic' public sphere of contestation where different hegemonic political projects can be confronted. This is, in my view, the sine qua non for an effective exercise of democracy.
>
> (Mouffe, 2005, p. 3)

McLean (1970) dismissed the concept of dissent as a prerequisite of a democratic society. He argues that 'the preservation and viability of a democratic order is intimately tied to a clear recognition of what dissent is permissible and what dissent is not', warning that a failure to recognise this and to make 'the necessary and qualitative decisions required' may result in the demise of democratic order (Ibid, p. 443). Unpicking the idea of responsible dissent, Platt (1971, p. 42) argued that characterising dissent as responsible or irresponsible on the basis of psychological criteria where responsible dissent is seen as motivated by the will to promote the well-being of society and where irresponsible dissent rises from a lesser motive entails the fallacy of *ad hominem* argument, moving from the question of the problems to an attack of the dissenter's motives, which also involves previous judgement regarding the moral value of any motivations. He warned against the assumption that there are certain 'pure facts' that policies are based on or that they play a crucial role in the decision-making process. Mouffe (2005, p. 82) proposed that the idea that politics have a purpose 'to establish consensus on one single model' removes the possibility of legitimate dissent. She claims that legitimate political channels for the facilitation of dissenting voices are crucial to prevent antagonistic conflicts.

In their exploration of how the protests have been policed in the UK since 1980s, Foot and Livingstone (2022, n.p.) find that

> by 2019 peaceful protests had become the subject of large-scale police operations. The strategy of undermining dissent reached a new peak with the alliance between Home Secretary Priti Patel and Commissioner Cressida Dick. In 2019 Dick wrote to Patel suggesting, 'In light of the challenges posed by this year's Extinction Rebellion protests, there are opportunities for much-needed legislative change to update the Public Order Act 1986'.

Despite the concerns raised by Amnesty International UK and Human Rights campaigners, the UK government remained determined to silence and eradicate protests. In 2019, the protesters were met with a blanket London-wide ban against protest, as the Home Secretary Priti Patel was keen to see 'unlaw-ful' protesters arrested. The High Court found that the ban itself was in clear breach of the law (Foot & Livingstone, 2022). Unfortunately, this did not im-pact the government's position, and the UK witnessed the story repeating it-self again and again. A Network for Police Monitoring report into the policing of the Black Lives Matter UK protests found that the police used excessive force, baton charges, horse charges, pepper spray, and violent arrests (Ibid). The Home Secretary's eagerness to squash the protests and see the protesters arrested was noted in every conversation with the participants and organisers of the protests discussed in this book. In her speech on 1st January 2022, the Home Secretary announced that cracking down on eco-protesters was one of her main priorities for the year, as she claimed it was vital that the govern-ment's Police and Crime Bill passed through parliament. Early in 2022, La-bour Party outright accused Priti Patel of being partly responsible for the lack of public's trust in the police. This coincided with Metropolitan Commissioner Cressida Dick's resignation after the Mayor of London made clear that he had no confidence in her following the scandalous police handling of the case of Sarah Everard, with revelations of officers bragging about violence towards women and exchanging racist and Islamophobic messages (Syal, 2022). In March 2022, the High Court ruled that the Metropolitan police breached the rights of the organisers of Sarah Everard's vigil.

> These attempts to undermine police leadership and ensure a more enforce-ment and power-driven model reflect the same desire to show who is in control and who has the power. These are not dynamics of liberal democ-racies; they pamper to those who are looking for simpler models of social control.
>
> (Jarman, 2021, p. 111)

Reicher (2022) uses Cop26, the UN Climate Change Conference held in Glasgow in November 2021 as an example of a successful implementation of rights-based policing. Rights-based policing is organised around defending the right to freedom of peaceful assembly as protected by the Article 11 of the European Convention of Human Rights and Article 21 of the International Covenant on Civil and Political Rights. *Adapting to Protest*, a major report was published by HM Inspectorate of Constabulary in 2009, suggesting new policing practices such as focusing on helping the crowd to achieve their law-ful goals instead of stopping them and dialogue policing, where police liaison officers take the mediator role between the police and the protesters. The future of the policing of protests should be based on rethinking of traditional polic-ing practices, not reinstating the police as a tool of repression. Unfortunately, the new Police and Crime Bill is a step backwards as instead of positioning the police as facilitators of dissent, it 'delegitimates protest in the eyes of the police, and delegitimates police in the eyes of protesters' (Reicher, 2022, n.p.).

In the UK, the police are trialling an AI-based program National Data Analytics Solution, which endeavours to determine how likely a person is to commit a crime or to become a victim of one. Although the police insist that they would not take action against any individuals identified by this program, the questions over the rights and privacy issues involved in the application of such programs remain. On the flip side, the wide range of malicious uses of AI and AI-driven tools by both individuals and organised criminal networks, hostile governments, hackers, and others create another worrying dimension, where even experts anticipate difficulties in distinguishing between what is authentic and fake and raise concerns over AI's impacts on the integrity of democratic processes (Engelke, 2020). Weak or absent accountability of the governments, states, and institutions leads to a crisis of legitimacy where many people see street protests as the only opportunity to express their opinions and feelings (Bleiker, 2008). Bleiker (2008, p. 38) challenges the fierce defenders of order, arguing that 'existing orders tend to be accepted as good and desirable because they reflect the values and institutions that have emerged slowly over time' and are seen as essential to maintain law and democracy; however, many injustices occur and result not from the absence of order but from an 'unjust order' and 'from the meticulous infatuation with an order'.

> BLM demonstrations have shown how protest has the capacity to bring dramatic change. After highlighting the one-sided presentation of history, this movement has achieved cultural change, including an unofficial rewrite of many educational curricula in the absence of government-authorised change. BLM achieved more over a few single days than the government-sponsored diversity programme had managed over years.
>
> (Foot & Livingstone, 2022, n.p.)

Attraction and engagement of the activist and supporters through the social movements' physical and online visibility as well as the general public perception of social movements and protest events can all be managed by using and manipulating traditional and modern communication methods, while the emergence of new media forms and social media provide new ways to spread and share information and to evoke strong emotional responses (Broniecki & Hanchar, 2017; Fawkes, 2007; Wanless, 2017). Through the global computer network, the Internet has become a space where social interactions and events take place, enabling new forms of relationships, communication, mobilisation, and learning which previously would have been unimaginable.

References

Abderrahim, L. and Gutiérrez-Colón Plana, M. (2021) A theoretical journey from social constructivism to digital storytelling. *The EuroCALL Review*, 29 (1), pp. 38–49.

BBC (2022) What is the police and crime bill and how will it change protests? *BBC* [Online], 28 April. Available:<www.bbc.co.uk/news/uk-56400751> [Accessed 10 September 2023].

Bleiker, R. (2008) The politics of change: Why global democracy needs dissent. *Georgetown Journal of International Affairs*, 9 (2), pp. 33–39.

Broniecki, P. and Hanchar, A. (2017) Data innovation for international development: An overview of natural language processing for qualitative data analysis. In: *Proceedings of the 2017 international conference on the Frontiers and Advances in Data Science (FADS)*, 23–25 October. Xian: IEEE.

Burrell, G. and Morgan, G. (1979/2005) *Sociological paradigms and organisational analysis: Elements of the sociology of corporate life* (Reprint). Aldershot: Ashgate Publishing Limited.

Engelke, P. (2020) *AI, society, and governance: An introduction* [Online]. Atlantic Council. Available from: <www.jstor.org/stable/resrep29327> [Accessed 15 October 2023].

Fawkes, J. (2007) Public relations models and persuasion ethics: A new approach. *Journal of Communication Management*, 11, pp. 313–331.

Foot, M. and Livingstone, M. (2022) 'Charged': How the police try to supress protest. *Huck* [Online], 23 May. Available from: <www.huckmag. com/article/charged-how-the-police-try-to-suppress-protest> [Accessed 14 October 2023].

Gerbaudo, P. (2020) The pandemic crowd: Protests in the time of COVID-19. *Journal of International Affairs*, 73 (2), pp. 61–76.

Herman, E.S. and Chomsky, N. (1988) *Manufacturing consent: The political economy of the mass media*. New York: Pantheon Books.

Jarman, R. (2021) Power, politics and policing: How the pandemic has highlighted fractures and fault lines in our society. *Journal of Global Faultlines*, 8 (1), pp. 100–113.

Latour, B. (2005) *Reassembling the social*. Oxford: Oxford University Press.

Mclean, E.B. (1970) Limits of dissent in a democracy. *Il Politico*, 35 (3), pp. 443–456.

Melucci, A. (1995) Individualization and globalization: New frontiers for collective action and personal identity. *Hitotsubashi Journal of Social Studies*, 27, pp. 129–142.

Mouffe, C. (2005) *On the political*. London: Routledge.

Pinckney, J. and Rivers, M. (2020) Sickness or silence: Social movements adaptation to COVID-19. *Journal of International Affairs*, 73 (2), pp. 23–42.

Platt, T.W. (1971) The concept of responsible dissent. *Social Theory and Practice*, 1 (4), pp. 41–51.

Reicher, S. (2022) I study crowds – that's why I know the police and crime bill will make us less safe. *The Guardian* [Online], 18 January. Available from: <www.theguardian.com/commentisfree/2022/jan/18/study-crowds-police-crime-bill-less-safe-priti-patel> [Accessed 14 October 2023].

Ryan, G.W. and Bernard, H.R. (2003) Techniques to identify themes. *Field Methods*, 15 (1), pp. 85–109.

Saunders, M., Lewis, P. and Thornhill, A. (2012) *Research methods for business students*. 6th Edition. London: Pearson Prentice Hall.

Snodgrass J.G., Clements K.R., Nixon W.C., Ortega C, Lauth S, and Anderson M. (2020) An Iterative Approach to Qualitative Data Analysis: Using Theme, Cultural Models, and Content Analyses to Discover and Confirm a Grounded Theory of How Gaming Inculcates Resilience. *Field Methods*, 32 (4), pp. 399–415.

Syal, R. (2022) Priti Patel partly responsible for lack of trust in police, says Labour. *The Guardian* [Online], 13 February. Available: <https://www. theguardian.com/politics/2022/feb/13/priti-patel-partly-responsible-for-lack-of-trust-in-police-says-labour-yvette-cooper> [Accessed 14 October 2023].

Wanless, A. (2017) A Participatory Propaganda Model. *Social Media & Social Order, Culture Conflict 2.0* [Online], Available from: <https://www. academia.edu/37951615/A_Participatory_Propaganda_Model_SM_pdf> [Accessed 7 June 2021].

6 Final remarks – in conversation with . . .

Over the last five chapters, we have investigated the mediation of protest events. We have addressed the contribution critical event studies can make in the investigation of social movements/coalitions, seeking to either change or to sustain a prevailing hegemonic perspective associated with an issue. While events of protest have been discussed within many fields, including sociology (Gøtzsche-Astrup, 2022), cultural and media studies (Teresa, 2022), and critical geography (Dufour, 2021), critical perspectives within event studies have only recently begun to consider the contribution they can make (Mowatt, 2020).

A key aspect of mainstream event studies is a consideration of the attendee experience. That is an area that has received scant attention within other aspects of social movements research. In the introduction, we mentioned the Advocacy Coalition Framework (ACF) of Paul Sabatier (Sabatier & Weible, 2019). A significant element of that was the ontological stability of the core of a coalition and the ephemerality of those associated with its periphery. How one supports those engaged with activism and seeks to protect those close to its ontological core from the vulnerabilities one becomes open to when engaged in events of dissent is an ongoing task of protest movements, but one that is rarely addressed.

The dialogues that have formed the pulse of our book's narrative share insights from the use and impact of the mediation of protest not just on how the event is articulated but also on how those close to a coalition's core can be affected by that mediation at both an organisational and, importantly, a personal level. The way the mediation of protest events impacts the individual is another area where critical event studies can facilitate insights not commonly being addressed in those other fields investigating social movements. The lived narratives of the life-world (Santos, 2015) for those at a coalitions ontological core often go unheard. It is for that reason we wanted to conclude our book with their voices, not ours.

Pete Knapp, of Scientist for Extinction Rebellion, and Jamie Klingler (one of the organisers of the Sarah Everard vigil) have, very generously, given their time to share some of their experiences of being an activist and the

DOI: 10.4324/9781003460640-7

relationship between media and activism. While their experiences are different, as are their perspectives on the role and impact of mediated messages with regards to events of dissent, both articulate clearly that the power and significance of how those mediated messages are framed are something of which social movements need to be conscious. Due to other commitments on their time, we were unable to meet them together. What follows, as the final remarks of our book, is an edited transcript of two separate conversations: the first with Pete and the second with Jamie.

In conversation with Pete Knapp

Ian R Lamond: Let's begin with a round of introductions. We'll begin with Giedre, then myself, and then Pete – if you go last you'll get a sense of what kind of things we're saying.

Giedre Kubiliute: OK, I'll start. Activism is a personal interest for me – I grew up in Lithuania during the 1990s with the singing revolutions and the fight for independence. So to me, protest had always been a part of my life and part of the lives of the people around me. During COVID, during the pandemic, when the protests with Black Lives Matter, Extinction Rebellion, Reclaim These Streets became more visible, I thought it was a perfect opportunity to pursue my interest. I was just about to pick a subject for my master's research project in event management, and it just seemed like a perfect topic. That's how I got involved with this topic, and, working with Ian, we ended up working on a book about it.

Ian R Lamond: Thanks, Giedre. I'm a senior lecturer researcher in critical event studies at Leeds Beckett University, and I have been involved in some form of non-violent and arts-based activism, associated with environmentalism, human rights, LGBTQIA+ rights, and anti-war protests, since my mid to late teens. So, quite some time. Protest, and particularly creative forms of dissent, have been something that's interested me for a very long time. When I became an academic, within the field of events research, I immediately gravitated to that side of events rather than the more corporate, or commercially orientated aspects of events. When Giedre did her research on protest, I was excited to find that there was somebody else who was as interested in these kind of topics and themes as myself. Pete, we are both looking forward to conversation today, and it's now over to you.

Pete Knapp:	Thank you. My name is Pete Knapp, and I'm a PhD candidate in the field of air quality at the Imperial College in London. And I have been quite heavily involved in activism related to Scientists for Extinction Rebellion, mainly. This has culminated in significant involvement in non-violent direct-action protest, which has, in certain circumstances, led to my arrest. Along with others, I have created a group called Imperial Climate Action, which is a campaign group designed to engage with the College in terms of policies related to food, transport, and relationships with fossil fuel companies. I'm happy to engage with groups who are trying to understand how protest groups work, with an aim to improve the rate of change that environmental activist groups can have. That is why I'm happy to contribute to this book chapter, in this way and in any other way.
Ian R Lamond:	Awesome. Thank you. I've used the term activist and apply it to myself, but I know some people that feel uncomfortable with that kind of label. Do you feel comfortable with it or is it something you find problematic?
Pete Knapp:	It's a very good question. I think those in academia tend to fall either side of being happy to be labelled as an activist and those who are not. To me, those who find the label of activist problematic are those that fear that a greater connection between being emotionally driven will mean they will lack the impartiality and apolitical nature that they suppose that science has. Academics, especially in the sciences, are trained to divorce their emotional connection with their work, and, in doing so, they find that the values attributed to their work are unemotional. In engaging with the environmental implications of excessive fossil fuel use to be devoid of an emotional connection leads to semi engagement with the reality. Therefore, I would say, those scientists or academics who are happy to label themselves as activists are more emotionally engaged in the consequences of extreme climate change and the consequences of inaction. Saying that, I also know some scientists and academics who are struggling to accept a label of being an activist because of the transition in their emotional engagement with the consequences of climate change.
Ian R Lamond:	Are you quite comfortable with that label yourself?
Pete Knapp:	Yes, I'm. I'm happy with the term, and I'm also aware that certain doors in the world of academia have been closed

to me by using that label. But I think in pushing for the kinds of urgent and high impact change that's required; it is inevitably going to result in certain doors being closed. I'm OK with that, although there is a balance to be struck by how many doors and which doors are closed.

Ian R Lamond: What drew you into activism?

Pete Knapp: It was whilst I was living and working in Beijing. I saw how extreme air pollution affected people who had no awareness of the causes and the barriers to change. Many people in Beijing knew that air pollution was bad but had no empowerment or sense of control in reducing the air pollution. They didn't know where it came from, and they didn't know the death toll that would result from this. While I was working in a school there, I saw many children suffering. Falling sick due to the air pollution. Some to an extent that they were so allergic to things that they had to walk around wearing what amounted to a beekeeper's suit. Going to the cinema, you'd have to wear a face mask. Going to a restaurant you'd have to wear a face mask. Even among expatriates, this became an accepted way of life, because they too felt unable to make any change, and they also didn't have the awareness of the scale of the issue. I understood then that politics had failed. The citizens of Beijing, and I, understood as well that the what was feeding into that was the greed of the West. This is where I saw a connection between high consuming behaviours in Europe, the States, Australia, and so on, with the hidden costs of mortality among countries who had no idea what was happening. These are hidden costs that are deliberately obscured by businesses who make money out of those chains. I was unaware of the willingness of certain individuals to subscribe to this way of running an economy, and I became aware of the environmental and human cost of capitalism. When I returned to the UK I was, I became, a lot more aware of the influence of corrupt government within the UK itself and became a little more politically engaged. This led to my involvement in Scientists for Extinction Rebellion, which started soon after I returned from China. When I started my PhD, I was living in Bristol, but when I came to London, where a lot of activity was situated, I got more involved in activism and direct action.

Ian R Lamond: Thank you. That sparked a couple of thoughts in my mind, as you were talking. I'm not sure which order I'll take them in, but I'll begin with what I wrote down first. The way you were talking about people's experience of a situation, and their awareness of the actual causes of it, put me in mind of early stages of modern medicine. When the idea of fighting bacteria and germs started to take root, it was a huge paradigm shift in how people thought about what caused illness and disease and a move away from establishing a balance of the body's four humours. There was much more consideration given to hygiene and making sure things were sterile. That huge paradigm shift resulted in quite seismic shifts within how people within the medical profession understood themselves. Their role in society and the world in general. Do you feel it's that similar kind of size of seismic shift that people are going through when they come to realise just what is behind what's going on?

Pete Knapp:

I think in the case of disease, the reaction or the paradigm shift was a reactive one. It reacted to mass death. We are in a position now where we're using the same reactive model which is not to act until there's mass death. With this kind of model, we will see global destabilisation and enormous costs to the biosphere. To shift the paradigm proactively is the challenge of the day. It has proved to be extremely difficult because the business of politicians, managing the economy, is all based on a reactive model. To be proactive means to accept costs before they're presented. The politicians have an allergic response to this because they think it is too difficult to translate proactivity into a message which the public will accept, but I think that inherently disrespects the public's ability to think proactively. Ultimately it is a failure of our political model, which is, to some extent, more like a dictatorship than a democracy. It seems to me that decisions are made unaccountably by a minority; by people who are easily influenced by powerful, vested interests, rather than a more open democracy, one which is citizen led. So, we need to shift the system to be more involving of citizens. But how? We either have to wait for a civil war or we involve citizens before that stage. The problem is, as far as I can tell, the efforts towards a more democratic and citizen led system are not a priority of the current government and, it seems to be, not a priority for the Labour Party either. Proportional representation, I think, and I think going in that direction are most important.

Ian R Lamond: The kind of 'democracy' you've been talking about is very much akin to that developed by Joseph Schumpeter, in 1942 (Schumpeter, 2010). In that he presents a model of democracy, which was basically about how the electorate elects people in to have a position of power. But once they've been elected to that position of power, the people step away and just leave those in power to do what they need to do until the next time they get to elect somebody else to take power. This differs from more contemporary writers like Chantelle Mouffe and Ernest Laclau (2014), and others, who argue that democracy should be more about participation and engagement from the bottom up. The other thing that that sort of triggered in my mind when you were talking earlier was to do with the economic model of growth that we currently have as a dominant frame of reference within modern liberal democracies, and most other economies, where gross domestic product, GDP, is used as the key measure of how economies are described as being 'successful'. Is that, pardon the pun, 'fuelling' the crisis, and do we need a different frame of reference if we really want to address the climate crisis?

Pete Knapp: Absolutely. The economy-focused society that we're living in is a direct result of colonialism and is inherently unsustainable. It will reach a limit. Not only will raw materials become impossibly scarce, but also the environmental cost, and the impact that has on societies, is not fact factored in. Certain things, like nature, are not seen as having a value in such an economic model until they are chopped down or they are destroyed, exploited or extracted. It's a system that will fail and it is failing. GDP is usually used as a measure of country's success, but that doesn't include the happiness or contentment, the well-being, of a population. It doesn't include the any element of sustainability. If we were to look at the most sustainable, most content groups, they have a very, very, low GDP. But I would argue that that is a much more successful group. So yeah; using GDP as a measure is one part of a big system which is failing.

  And I would also add that every economic model that you get from academic journals tends not to include much of the climate science or the trajectories of likelihoods of bread basket failures, mass migration, or civil wars that relate to the extraction.

So even contemporary academic journals of economics, which feed into the insurers of the world and the banking world, are flawed. They only tell half the story. Their talk of success is in terms that relate to a neocolonial attitude, one which is pervasive even today. It is a discourse of extracting minerals from Africa or South America and using those resources to feed populations of high consumption from across the world.

It exacerbates inequality and creates poverty. But this kind of economic model is reaching its limit. Governments around the world that rely on that model alone means that when that model fails the societies that rely on those models will also fail. In the UK, when we will see extreme weather making certain homes flooded and uninsurable, house prices in these areas will crash. House price has such a high link to the wealth of those in the country. Instability in house prices will have huge knock on effects on people's ability to live their way of life. But we're also living in a way which is totally reliant on how much money you have. Relying on all that is a recipe for disaster, and until we can change our value system, and our resilience, society will remain vulnerable to collapse.

Ian R Lamond: Protest then has a role to play in articulating counter positions and counter orientations. Giedre now has a few questions she'd like to ask you about that and media's representation of protest.

Giedre Kubiliute: Sure. Arguably the role of media was there to inform society. Now the focus seems to have shifted from informing to entertaining, whilst also broadcasting a certain broad political perspective and sustaining a narrow range of economic interests. What do you feel is the role of media in the activist world? Does it have any redeeming qualities? Is it just there to squash the activism and disempower people? What is your view on the media, both traditional and digital?

Pete Knapp: This is an enormous area. The media has the potential to manipulate people's understanding of reality. I mean, the media have been used so frequently in dictatorships as a way to control the narrative. I think it has been shown that all accents in Russia are now very similar because of the dominance of the Russian radio in disseminating ideas across the whole country in order to stabilise it (REF); to prevent it from falling into societal collapse. So in terms of bringing everyone on to sing from the same hymn sheet, centralised media is essential. However, it is currently totally vulnerable too, being manipulated by vested interests. We're seeing so many of the defences that the fossil fuel industry use being echoed by people that are reading newspapers and watching TV news, and more recently people online and on social media.

We know that the private media is essentially controlled by the people who have the most money, and the people who have the most money are going to be the people who extract and exploit the most. This results in a population who believe that everything they hear in the media. It is presented as all they need to know, especially when it comes from trusted sources. But public service broadcasting is also fragile and worried about its own existence. If it were to seriously upset politicians, they would have their platform removed. So, in a sense, they feel they have to appease politicians to ensure their survival. That makes them vulnerable to. Consequently, it echoes narratives that appease politicians that have been corrupted by vested interests. So, even public service broadcasting is open to manipulation, although very few members of the public are accepting of this manipulation of their narrative. Even reporters from such broadcast media, or the more liberal press, believe that they are able to say what they want. This is frustrating because it shows that the journalists are unaware of the boundaries that are imposed on them. I mean it's subtle. I'm not aware of very many journalists who feel that they are self-censored. And many, if not all, journalists are. This self-censorship in a sense comes from the general world of journalism and what is within the Overton window (Beck, 2010) of what you can talk about.

There are also people who are victims of the atomisation of society, unable to engage with the local community to get the support that they need to feel heard and feel empowered. Without that sense of community, people rely on news media much more than they ever would do if they had support from their local communities. Media capitalises on this vulnerability of people. Consequently, it tends therefore to be the people who are most vulnerable that become the most vocal when it comes to xenophobia or racism, or homophobia or, to a lesser extent, perhaps voting for Brexit. People who are manipulated much more by the media tend to, I think, be the people who have been failed most by society, even though they may not know it. This is why I engage with some of those news sources. Not because I support them – I wouldn't advise anyone support them – but it is important to engage with them. To my mind, it's the only way to engage the demographic that consumes those sources. They won't go to a protest or listen to a speech that I'm giving on the street. They'd be infuriated by a video on Twitter (now X) of people blocking a road. But any engagement with that demographic to me is like gold dust. By engaging with it, well, it feels to me as though that is the only way to engage with this group. So when I'm interviewed on such channels, I don't talk to the interviewer I talk to the audience, and I accept that.

We have different opinions, but I try to establish that what we all have in common, and this is to counteract the atomisation of society. We have reached a point where fridge companies sell a fridge to every home, car companies will sell a car to every home, and so on – everyone has one of everything, and no one shares anything. All this atomisation is just to perpetuate an unsustainable economic mode, one that values selling more crap simply to increase GDP, and always at the cost of those who are living rough. My way of trying to rebalance that is to engage with the right-wing media, and it cost me emotionally. But I feel that it is important nonetheless.

Giedre Kubiliute: Your answer kind of leads into my next question. I'm sure most of the activists are aware of the power of the media, the filters and frames it uses to 'inform' people about protest. Are there any ways from your point of view that activist could actually either alter that message, based on a knowledge how the media works, or do something differently to make the media work for them.

Pete Knapp: The media forces activism into spaces which put the activist at risk; it will only report actions of those who are being arrested. Consequently, it forces extreme activism because that's the only way it will be reported. We tested this with *The Big One* in London in April this year. Over 100,000 people were on the streets in London, and it didn't get reported. Because we know that any kind of peaceful protest that is inclusive doesn't make the headlines. We know what does make the headlines is people putting themselves at risk. But that then alienates people from being involved in that kind of activism. Some people cannot take those risks. For example people who rely on visas; people who are relying on benefit payments; who don't have the time because they are single parents; people who don't have the ability to get involved because of physical disabilities. It becomes incredibly difficult and especially for people of colour to be involved because of the way that the media represents them. It forces successful activism to come at a personal cost, which many people can't take. This results in the white middle class being seen as the only people able to shift the dial, because only they can cope with the costs that the media are forcing on engaging with protest. But this, then, becomes a self-perpetuating issue, and it's very, very, difficult then to involve groups where there are perceived barriers to getting involved. If the media were more responsible, they would allow activism to be more accessible to people of different backgrounds. But as it stands, their representation perpetuates an inequality within activism itself.

Ian R Lamond: That mediate pushing for more extreme manifestations of activism not only alienates people from direct engagement but also feeds into a political discourse that supports legislation around its control.

Pete Knapp: Yeah, this is the police sentencing and courts bill, which was, effectively, a result of pressure that was created by vested interest in the media. Yeah, in a way it's a way of making protest illegal. It also forces many out of the ability to be active. That then means that people feel even more disempowered than they were before. It stokes the flames of inequality and civil unrest. That's how the right-wing support grows and opens the door to fascism. So, to me, it's leading us down a very dangerous path towards fascism.

Giedre Kubiliute: Last time we spoke, you mentioned that there's very little understanding of the difference between supporting the movement and supporting the cause; that many people don't really support protests, or activist groups and disruptive action, but they support the cause behind it. I wondered if you could expand a bit more on that.

Pete Knapp: This goes back to what I was saying about the Overton window. It sets the boundaries of what people will accept. When you move that boundary, the reasoning of what is acceptable in public shifts. We're seeing this both in hard right policy and the lies of politicians, which are becoming more regular and, therefore, shifting what people think is acceptable. But also in things like diet. For example, when people say now that they are vegan, and to a greater extent than we've had before, supermarkets have a rationale for stocking vegan food lines, and in restaurants, menus have green boxes around their vegan meals. We see a shift in what is the extreme, and it shifts the Overton window. In the case of activism, you need to shift the Overton window, though this is inherently going to be a minority position. It's the edge of edges of a normal distribution, it broadens it, shifts it, though it will inevitably only include a tiny proportion of people who support it. But what it does is it moves the median. That's where the bulk of people are. So most don't have to agree with the extreme – but it shifts what they think is normal. That is why I would support the more extreme forms of direct action. Even though I know many people don't support it, that's not the point. The point is to move the extreme so that by doing that, you're shifting the mode and the median of the population.

Ian R Lamond: We nearing the end of the window we've given ourselves for this conversation, and it's been really interesting. Thank you so much. I wondered, if you felt comfortable to do so, if you could say something briefly about how participating in the activism can impact someone's mental health?

Pete Knapp: Mental health and activism is an extreme danger for people who don't navigate this correctly. If activism is taken on your own or if it's done among groups who themselves are governed in a way which is vulnerable, then that can lead people down into areas which are dangerous. Poor mental health associated with activism is mainly affected by isolation. In terms of climate action, it's very easy to be the only person in your immediate vicinity, or your friendship group or your family, who is engaging with this. The only way to protect your mental health, within activism, is to join groups of people who are doing the same thing. On your own it's a one-way ticket to the poor mental health, and, in the most severe cases, it could be a one-way ticket to suicide. This is a real danger. It's also a problem when working with those who are vulnerable, because they can be easily misled – encouraged to sign up to things that they're not emotionally equipped to deal with. So it's very, very, important in activist circles to always have the door open for exit, if you need to. This is very different to the way that cults work, which is where the door is firmly closed and anyone wandering towards that door is ushered back. So, in activist circles, the exit must always be open, and people directed there if it's clear that they need to leave. It allows people to get out of a situation even when they are unaware of being unable to cope with themselves. If other people can see that that's the case, and that's happened with me when I've got to an extreme point in activism, I've been told to take a step back. In a cult, I would be given a greater platform and told to get more involved.

So it's very important to consider mental health in climate activism – and to recognise the commonalities with those getting involved with activism and those getting involved with right-wing extremism; which is feeling alone, feeling disempowered, feeling like a society has failed and that you have no control. If those qualities are what lead people down either path, I think it's very important to engage with people who are suffering this. Engaging them in a way that is constructive and helpful for their mental health, unlike a cult – that would be very damaging.

But there is something I forgot to mention about the media is that applies in a very, very, similar sense to academia. That is, until journalists cry about climate change, they will never be able to report it. Likewise, until academics cry about climate change, they should never be writing about it. This is at one of the big obstacles in both academia and in journalism. There is a deliberate barrier between your emotional engagement and your academic engagement. To me, that is why so much of academia writing and so much journalism is in the state that it's in.

Ian R Lamond: So, despite the intentions of some parts of that community, they still reinforced the issues that are creating the problem.

Pete Knapp: Yeah.

Ian R Lamond: We will end our conversation there. Thank you so much for your openness, your honesty, your directness. We really value your contribution, and I'm sure Giedre will join me in that. From the deepest part of ourselves, for what you've shared with us today, thank you.

Giedre Kubiliute: Yeah, absolutely.

Pete Knapp: It's a pleasure.

~||~

In conversation with Jamie Klingler

Giedre Kubiliute: I think Jamie's experience, from previous conversation, has been different from other activists and other movements I've spoken with, in that you found that media was very positive in terms of support for the movement and the event. So, my questions are about the role media can play in activism, and specifically what was its role in Sarah Everard's vigil? I know you mentioned in the past that it kind of fuelled the whole outcry. But why do you think that? What specifically was media's role in the whole story?

Jamie Klingler: I don't think you can underestimate the whiteness in all of it. The fact that I was white, the fact that Sarah was white, the fact that Sarah worked in media, the fact that it was a London-centric story, the fact that most women in the media there knew somebody who knew Sarah. Media is quite insular. The fact that I worked in the media, albeit I worked in the publishing side rather than broadcasting side, but it meant I understood the mechanics of how PR works. Me and my group said yes to every interview, with the exception of more right-wing broadcasters. We made ourselves incredibly available. Personally, I did 87 interviews, I think, that weekend. We made ourselves that available, and that open, and that critical. Once I was on camera for the first time, I realised that all the training from when I was a kid in mock trial, and all the debates, and all that, really came in handy. I mean, a lot of interviews here are really innocuous and they've got so much time to fill. We were also in that witching hour where we were mid-pandemic, but also Times Radio had just started. So we had LBC, we had Times Radio, we had BBC, and we had Sky, and they are all on 24-hour broadcasting schedules. We were on all of them all of the time. So, like I did LBC every day for weeks. I did Times Radio every day for weeks.

They have rules about not being the guest about the same subject three times, but we had enough people that we were rotating each other in and making sure that we were in every single interviewing opportunity. We didn't curse and we were well-spoken, middle-class, white women. And so when you're talking about who they want to project to Middle England, who are relatable, and news stories like this don't happen to people like us, and people like us are the people they were broadcasting to. So we were pushing on a pretty open door. The specifics of the case being as horrific as they were – the perpetrator being a serving police officer, who was also white. But just that, he was an armed serving police officer that his colleagues nicknamed *the rapist*, the fact that her family and all of her friends had been on the news so much, and her picture had been everywhere. That it was Clapham; you know, everybody that comes to London for three years from Middle England comes to Clapham, finds a spouse and then moves back out to Middle England. And so it holds a part of the country and a part of the interest of the country, and she did everything right. The thing is women of colour get that coverage. Nobody gets the coverage that Sarah Everard got. Women of colour would get less than one-fourth of that, even when they got pictured on the front pages.

My mission over the last two and half years has been to amplifying those voices. To meet with Mina Smallmen (whose two adult daughters were murders by two former police officers in 2020) and Zara Aleena's family (who was stalked, sexually assaulted, and murdered in 2022 by Jordan MacSweeny – who had been recently released from prison for crime committed before 2006) – being there and being a conduit to conveying interview requests to their families and to their spokespeople. I'm really conscious of the fact that my blinders were on until Sarah was killed. Janome from Sisterspace asked me on a Times Radio interview, why did it take a white woman being killed for my blinders to come off? And she's absolutely right, it's because Sarah was like me – I identified with Sarah, and that's what took the blinders off. And I've not yet been able to put those blinders back on; I haven't really tried. It is a painful reminder that black communities and minority communities in the UK are over policed and underserved and have been screaming about it since the beginning of time. They are ignored; regularly, regularly, ignored. In my own very little way, when I was interviewed the first weekend that Mark Rowley (London's police commissioner) was in power, and they were asking me what his number one priority should be, well, they fully expected me to come on and say women's safety, and I said justice for Chris Kaba (illegally shot by a police firearms officer in October 2023). And so, in my own way, subverting what they expect a white woman to care about.

I think if refugee women, if women that are being traf-
ficked as sex workers, are being raped by police, then we
need to stand up for those women. For women that don't
speak English and are being abused by police and cannot speak out, white women can't even speak out about
the police. What are they doing to those women? I think
that it's all of us that are getting abused. Stuff has recently
come out about police that use sex workers being allowed
to stay on the force. It turned my stomach – there's no way
they're paying for those services. There is no way that
those police are not using their power for sexual gain; it
infuriates me and, to be honest, it boils my blood.

Ian R Lamond: So how do you think we turn that narrative, if it is still
dominated by white middle-class perspectives in the me-
dia, how do you go about changing that?

Jamie Klingler: I don't think that any of us, from the outside, can. There
are, basically, six black reporters that are put on black stories in this country, and they are literally only assigned
to black stories. Those stories not being treated as mainstream stories. There's a need for a real mix up in the
whole way that race is treated in this country. The country
must start to believe that they have as big of a problem
with racism as the States and other countries. There is no
recognition of the issues of race in this country, other than
black people shouting about it – it doesn't hit the sides.
The narrative around racism is just wrong. You've got a
white guy on the news yesterday saying that in Ipswich
Centre City Centre, no one is speaking English. I mean
98% of people in Ipswich are speaking English you know;
it's this narrative that is so racist. When you've got mainstream politicians rolling that out, the media is following that lead, then you've got the bids from the Telegraph
coming from further right-wing places, you know that that
swing is not something that I'm able to control.

But we definitely were media darlings and we were re-
corded. I do not, and have never had, any of the animosity
that Just Stop Oil or Extinction Rebellion or Black Lives
Matter have had. None of that came at us at all.

Giedre Kubiliute: You mentioned before that obviously you had experience
in the events industry, and you're aware of how media
works. So, do you think if you hadn't had that knowledge,
the story would have reached the media at the level it did,
and should other movements, perhaps, have somebody
with the knowledge of event management and the media,

so they can utilise that knowledge to reach the media and to communicate their narratives?

Jamie Klingler: I think our experiences with press were incredibly helpful. In immediately putting up a Gmail address and answering like every Gmail, having that joint account that we were all responding to, agreeing amongst ourselves that there would be set press lines – and those were the lines we were going to take and we were going to stick with them. I think the way we handled it was amazing, given the level of the challenge and the volume of media requests. It was really helpful for us to do it and do it well.

But there have been other times, like the interim report from the Casey Review[1] where I cleared two days of my schedule to do press and didn't get a single request. A Manchester Police officer was arrested for the attempted murder and rape of a woman in a Manchester hotel – I cleared my schedule to do press and there wasn't a phone call. No one knows his name, and it got buried. It's very, very hard to read what the story of the week, month, year, will be in the UK.

When the Casey interim report came out, and there was a female police officer saying that she was told that if she fell asleep during a night shift that was considered consent, I was already I had lines. I had everything ready to go and Jeremy Hunt became chancellor, so it didn't get any coverage. There was barely a blip. Even if you know the media and you know how it works, you know how silly season works, you know what's coming with 17 changes in government last summer, there is no way to actually predict what is going to run. You can't tell what will spark of the imagination of the British public, what's going to get its attention and what isn't. And that's really painful.

But Sarah was the perfect storm. It sounds awful, but we were able to capitalise on that. It really was an organic movement – we answered the call and we did it well. It wasn't as if we were pitching ourselves out to news stories. Literally everything we did was incoming, and everything we did was receptive, rather than us hiring an agency or me acting as a press agent.

With the rape survey that just came out, about survivors and how they were treated by police when they gave their stories, I worked with Katrin Hohl, from Soteria Bluestone, as a press agent to get that story out – their press agent was burying it. In that case I'm really proud of the work I did to get that into the press. But that was all outreach. It's a very different beast when it is producers buying and fighting for your time to be the person covering the story, or you trying to seed something and gather interest and gather producers' curiosity rather than responding. Gathering that context book. Gathering who I now know in media, even when they all move to other places, and keeping them on my phone. Them knowing that I will definitely answer the phone day or night means that I get stories out there, and I have a media profile and presence. But I don't have an agent – I don't do it that way. It's all been organic.

I do think it's useful, but I also don't know how organisations would pay for it, or fund it, or understand how useful it is because they wouldn't get the same response if it was, let's say, Black Lives Matter. I have trained young women, especially black young women, on how to do radio interviews – I could train them all day and night. But I can't promise they're going to get booked, because this country does not put people that don't look like me on air 14 times a day. That may sound like a cop out, but it's just the facts of the way things are treated here. You get cultural reporters who are the ones that are giving black stories, like Melissa Sagado in the Mirror, who's amazing, but she's only put on Black Caribbean and Asian stories. But it's also like her appointment is said like it's a special assignment. Like she should be honoured to get that assignment. But it also means Black Asian stories only get put in certain parts of the paper, covered by one reporter who happens to also be black. And so it's a constant reaffirmation of what they're doing, even though it's an awful way to report the news, and it's an awful way to continue reporting news.

Mina Smallman went to Stacy Dooley and said I need your audience to know about my girls. And that's how she got Stacy to do a documentary on her girls, and what the police did. Without Mina doing that outreach and talking to somebody who looks like Stacy, like Stacy's entire audience, that documentary would never have been made. How many mothers are like Mina? How many mothers are going to do what Mina did? Most of them would have no idea how to even start dealing with media. Sabina Nessa (who was murdered in 2021) is another where we fought to get her on the front pages, but her family doesn't do the media circus – they don't all speak English. There is a vigil, which gained some coverage, but nothing like the coverage it should, and the cycle just continues – they excuse themselves because it's like, oh, well, it's public interest but not enough of the public cares about it, so it's put on page 74.

It happens again, and again, and again. I don't know how you break those cycles of racism. I think it's a much bigger question than any of us can really solve.

Ian R Lamond: Most of what you've been mentioning has been about broadcast media or mass media. Is there an argument that goes along the lines that, given contemporary media consumption, which is much more platform based, and streaming, that news media is actually increasingly secondary and because of that, echo chambers within social media and digital media become dominant. How do we combat that?

Jamie Klingler: Well, part of what I'm so upset about is we could not have done *Reclaim* (Reclaim These Streets) without Twitter, and Twitter today would not have let *Reclaim* happen the way it happened or enable us to raise £600,000. The way we fought, and the way we held the police to account, would not happen in X. I don't know how to reach all of those people. I don't know how to reach all of those celebrities. I don't how to reach all of our support now. It's very upsetting and it's hard.

Ian R Lamond: One of the people we've been speaking to recently was suggesting that the prevailing hegemony within media is such that the only way you will get reported, other than being the right looking face, or the right class, etcetera, is if you do something extreme. That, they argue, leads to negative reporting which, in turn, leads to legislation to squash protests. What are your feelings around that kind of perspective?

Jamie Klingler: So this brings up stuff about Just Stop Oil and Extinction Rebellion, and the means they use. I struggle with it a bit. When you're pushing on an open door, if you do something destructive that goes against the values of the people that are on your side – are you then doing the opposite? So like I was on radio one night, and there was an environmental activist who glued his hand to the mic in the studio, and I was on next, so they just moved to the studio next door. I suppose it's a funny story. It's a bit of a like, oh, you screwed yourself there, type of thing. There was another one where somebody that was on Sky News sat on the floor during the interview, to make a point. Again, if you're doing the same thing, if you're speaking in the same tones, if you're acting the same way, you're not gathering the attention. Horrific crimes, like a serving police officer raping, murdering, and abducting that pretty young woman is just walking down the street, you know? So that was extreme enough to capture everyone's horror and imagination, but I don't really know if just doing more and more shocking things works when everything else seems to have jumped the shark. I mean, political satire doesn't make any sense anymore when the politicians are worse than anything that used to be on Veep or The Thick of It. And so when it's all 'comedy', when it's all the craziness of America and, you know, like we have lost a level of civility – we've lost a level of discourse that works. We've lost this ability with the police, and we've lost our right to protest because they've been able to villainize the likes of Extinction Rebellion, even though the world's on fire and there are floods and . . . It's like, *oh yeah, arrest the protesters that held up signs* when we're drowning, you know, like when the world is actually on fire, rather than giving them credit for trying to be chicken little and say the sky is falling, you know. Right this week, the whole thing about Greta and that her autistic octopus being anti-Semitic, you know. They will do anything to tear down a woman that has called attention to the fallacy and the failures of the free world for the last eight years. They will do anything to not give her credit for being who she is and standing up for what she stood up for, long before anybody else was doing it.

Giedre Kubiliute: I wanted to ask about activism and mental health. There seems to be increased focus on activist mental health and how people come to activism. And I know your route in was a sort of an accidental activism. Some may not be aware of the pressures and the stresses they're going to face as an activist. So I wanted to ask you, what were your experiences in terms of that?

Jamie Klingler: Well, it's not just stress and pressures, it's the threats. You know, it's like I've had, I think I've had five bouts of emergency counselling. The first was that first weekend because the anti-trans community came out and said we'd stolen money, and said horrible things about us, because we were giving the donated money to trans inclusive women's rights organisations. They found, like a shot of me in the Maldives and said I'd stolen money. We didn't have JustGiving attached to the money yet because we didn't mean to raise money, you know? And it was half a million. But it stayed in JustGiving. I mean there's a complete public paper trail, but even the public eye was like tapping noses and saying, where have all those pounds gone? What are they reclaiming with it?

It's still gonna make me cry. The night that we donated the £550,000 to Rosa[2] I had a picture of my dead mother and a non-alcoholic bottle of champagne posted saying that she would be proud, and they said I was a fame whore who made my name on Sarah's neck. And it's just still the most violent thing that's happened to me – these are supposed women's rights people. I'm a biological woman and I've had a fake OnlyFans account made of me and sent to my father. I've had death threats, I've had numerous, numerous penises sent to me, and there is no support. I have had a friend of mine who's an entrepreneur who's paid for me to have some trauma counselling over the last year. But you also have so many women coming to you with their rape stories, and I'm not trained in any of that.

The anniversary of Bibaa and Nicole's death (Mina Smallwood's daughters), the second anniversary, I spoke and a woman came up to me and said I need your help or my kids. Will my kids and I'll be dead in six months? She gave me a picture of her children. I've not done frontline, and there were women there that could do the frontline and to hand that off. But like, I was hysterical. I didn't, you know, and there's not . . . some of us, women that are on that level of exposure, we play trauma ping pong, and we compare our death threats. We compare, like jokingly – you know, gallows humour – about it, but we are the support for each other. We have fought the police, and we are the ones that privately have conversations. Nobody else gets it because nobody else has been on TV and had that amount of material shot at them.

There's not financial support, there's not mental health support. It burns you out quickly and heavily, you feel the weight of the world, and you feel responsible. I was about to go to a party a couple weeks ago and somebody had put me in touch with somebody who needed help. I thought it was about a historic case, but when I spoke to this woman, it turned out she worked in the police, and she was raped six years ago. There was a data breach, and she found out there had been four more victims – and he's still serving police officer. I escalated that to the mayor's office, and he has been suspended from duty. But one of the red tops caught wind of it and was going to publish it, with my name. I thought, I was gonna get myself killed because – he had raped women at work, so why would he not come after me? And we had to get all kinds of lawyers involved. That helps me pro bono because of how high profile it is, but he would have had my name.

There is not support, like who am I supposed to call for that? The Victims Commissioner does nothing; I mean, the Victims Commissioner has an active stalker for 22 years. She can't help anybody. She can't help herself. There are no actual routes to help most women. And that, coupled with knowing that I've had 110 thousandth of the impact that an Andrew Tate has had, you know? It's a drop in a bucket compared to the overwhelming misogyny that he is raining down, you know. But that's why I go to the university and give a lecture every year. Those girls write their papers, they're inspired by me, and they are so nice about telling you why and talking to you. You get actual tangible stuff that you can hold on to rather than just the big 'Oh my God, the sky is falling'. But no, nothing mental health wise. It has been a very, very difficult two and a half years. I made so much more money running National Burger Day than fighting for police reform and women's safety, even though it is so much more important.

Giedre Kubiliute: Do you feel that the backlash and the threats, in your opinion, were they targeted? Was there maybe not political interest; were there more people behind it, or do you think it was just the reaction of individuals? And, if it's just random people, why do you think?

Jamie Klingler: The TERFs (Trans-Exclusionary Radical Feminists) that came after us, that was very organised. They had 200 women donate us £5 and then demand it back because we were giving it to men with lipstick on. They're they are incredibly organised and incredibly vicious. The woman that did it to us is a barrister, so there is a respectability there. There is an absolute cruelty, and it's coming from women – it's more painful because it's organised *and* because it's coming from women. Actually, in my political journey, I would say that when I started this, my views on trans women were the weakest part of my politics. Now, if anything, they've pushed me so far the other way. If your hobby is about ruining the lives for such a small number of the population who have already been subjected to so much more in terms of, like . . . Look, I'm lucky I look how I look, I sleep with men, I wake up, and I can go on TV and feel comfortable, you know, let alone what trans people in this country go through. And then you're going to spend your entire hobby just trying to destroy them and to take them down – like, get a better hobby. I did nothing other than stand up and be counted and raise £500,000 for women. And you're going to make fun of my sobriety and my dead mother and act like it was some big career thing. I make less money than I've ever made in my life, and I work harder than I've ever worked. It is a myth that I am on some fame hungry joyride of activism.

I don't know if anyone has it easy that does any of this. It is a painful cause. It's the underbelly of society. You know, you're dealing with victims. You're dealing with people that have been shat upon from the highest heights, and you're trying to help. Nobody that's ever done any activism thinks it's luxurious.

Giedre Kubiliute: So how do you keep the drive with all the negativity that comes with activism? What continues to drive you?

Jamie Klingler: I was interviewed by a woman that was at UCL, and it was the weekend that the war in the Ukraine started. So we met, I had my dog with me, and we were chatting. After an hour of interviewing me about Reclaim These Streets I'm like, well, tell me about you. She said she had had a hard weekend because she was from Ukraine and I was like, what are you doing interviewing me? I was able to get her on Woman's Hour the next day. I give her some bylines – she got a byline in Harper's Bazaar. So I put her in touch with other people and mentor her, like, for every three months. I'd say I meet with a young woman, and I have, like, a number of young women students that I check in with because I need the face to face of younger women who are then going to carry the flag long after I'm done. As for my mental health – basically that I just got a puppy. Like, obviously I go to therapy, but I like, honestly, getting a puppy and checking out a bit, because it's all been too much. It's a lot, a lot of the time. He entertains me a lot. He's five months old this week.

Ian R Lamond:	I'd be interested to hear more about you talking about mentoring; that seems like an interesting progression.
Jamie Klingler:	It's not very structured, but I do quite a bit of media training as well. There was a young woman who was in a Premier Inn who is blind and was there on Guy Fawkes Night, and they came in her room and kicked her out. They thought she was faking blind and just had a dog in her room. And so I got in touch with her and was like training her. Now, for me it was a big learning – you see, the way I've decided to do my interviews on radio are like, I have three lines on my screen and anytime anybody wants to take me off of that, I keep them on my screen, that is what I need to keep the conversation on. Don't get distracted. With her I was like, I have no idea how to do that. If you can't look at your screen. So she typed it on her Braille machine, and she had them in front of her, so she could keep feeling it during her interviews.

And again, like getting young women to be more confident when they're gonna be interviewed, when their story is lighting up and they're getting that influx of producers asking them what they're doing – asking them if they'll come on, that's kind of where I excel. I kind of learned it by fire, so I reach out to a lot of those young women and train them on media, do some fake interview requests with them, and kind of get them ready so that they feel better when they're talking to producers. I also have a list of producers that are kind and will give them softballs and will help them, especially if they're neuro diverse. I'll do some pre interviews with them. Then it's taking a backseat. But it's also watching some people shine, and giving some people some more confidence when they're going to be doing things that are well out of their comfort zones. And so that stuff feels really good.

Giedre Kubiliute:	Do you think this is now your path for the future? Do you think you'll ever be able to step away from activism again?
Jamie Klingler:	I've tried to step back a few times, the most recent being after that article was about to run. I'm much better at being angry than I am scared, and that was a really scary weekend. But because I have not been a direct victim of the police, other than the protest stuff, and because I am not a survivor of sexual assault, I don't have trauma re-enactment every time I do interviews and every time I talk about it.

I found the David Carrick (a convicted serial rapist and former police officer) stuff, hugely, hugely damaging. Some details, like the detail of him starving her under her stairs. I gained 15 pounds that month because all I did was eat. I had food on me at all times, and it was something about him starving her that set up something in me; I had emergency counselling that month as well. Talking about those details, and trying to hide from them – I was so scared of what he had done. It's things like that which set you off and you're like, no, I need better work–life balance. I need to get back into industry and I need to do this 30% of my time, not 90% of my time.

It's isolating because reclaim (Reclaim These Streets) doesn't really exist anymore, in any form. Partially because of how damaging it was with getting attacked by TERFs at the very beginning. We never developed a bank account because we were scared of what else they were going to say about us stealing money. By not having a bank account it made it really clear none of us ever took any money. If anything, we donated money to get walkie talkies. We donated money for the tree, out of our own pockets, for Mina's children, you know. But knowing that you're going to be accused of theft. It is such a slap in the face. For me it's quite similar to when women lie about being raped because you are desecrating everyone who has had to live through these type of experiences.

Them saying we stole money was very, very, painful because a year and a half later, people are like, oh, but the money. And I'm like, I can literally show you, we had two crowdfunders for justice – we had one JustGiving that came from the public, and every single penny of that went to Rosa. Having to justify myself, when you have never done anything but good, is quite difficult.

It's been really difficult to then say that you're worth being paid, and set up the mechanics to be paid, without being scared that you're gonna get crucified or people are gonna just never believe you that you did it voluntarily. Unless you can absolutely never have a bank account and never take any money from your work. So it's poisonous, it's a poisonous atmosphere and, to be honest, those circles of women activists claiming that you're in it for the wrong reasons have been really painful too. But there's also so much friendly fire from the left – it's quite difficult to not burn out.

Giedre Kubiliute: You mentioned that you have a network of journalists and producers. In terms of activists, do you have a network of activists that support each other, or do you feel like you stand on your own, or is it as and when?

Jamie Klingler: There's definitely a bunch of us – we're in touch quite a bit, like with the court case that they just went through, so there's one-on-one, and there's a lot of the people that were kind of incidentally involved with what's happened with police reform that I'm now friends with, that I speak to regularly. We check in with each other a lot. I have gained amazing counsel from Amanda Reed, who's the head of the Women's Equality Party. She's been an absolute rock. Then there's Melissa Segado, from the Mirror, who is their main black reporter, she has a dog like mine – we bonded over our dogs. So when the issues that you're dealing with are this emotional, and they're affecting the reporter and producer, there's a different bond there. You know, I was media to begin with, I was in publishing, so I speak the language. I'm not precious about any of it. I'm available 24/7 and always up for a good spar on TV, the radio, you know – we've become friendly.

Ian R Lamond: Is there any risk of . . . I mean with the social media that's supported the movement early on and now, effectively closing down or being restricted in some way, what do you think is the impact of that?

Jamie Klingler: It couldn't happen today. It couldn't happen today.

Ian R Lamond: With the restrictions that are growing around producing in an increasing managed digital media, what would you say to somebody saying that there is the risk of producing celebrity activists – that the only activist that can be effective on such platforms will become those that can afford to promote and articulate a profile.

Jamie Klingler: I did a speech yesterday and got asked how do you start something and I think you start it in your community. You started at your church or your mom's group; if you care about something somebody else is gonna care about it. But it's finding those other people next door, you know. And I think the community and doing smaller things, really close to where you live, can make a difference. It can be really powerful and really progressive.

  Digitally, we are in a really rough place right now. I think celebrities are scared to get cancelled over all kinds of stuff. I did the UN Women UK Awards last year and it was right when Twitter was supposedly going to be turned off that weekend. And that was my direct line to all these people. I don't know their agents. I don't have their phone numbers. I only have the ability to DM them on Twitter and having that taken away was difficult. Having your verified thing taken away because people were impersonating me was painful. I also don't have an Only-Fans, unsurprisingly, but having an OnlyFans made of my face with another woman's genitalia was quite devastating. I'm worried about the 16-year-old who kills herself because stuff like that, you know. My way of coping with all of it is to make it not about me personally but a bigger cause – it is about all women. Then I'm able to fight back, when it's when it was just me and I was terrified. I'm much better when I'm able to be a warrior for other people. I'm much better at fighting for other people than when it's an individual thing about me. Then I get upset, and turn off the world for a while.

And that's the thing. When it's a personal attack, about my mom and me, or my drinking, I just couldn't fathom that. They think that's activism? It's punching down rather than punching up. And I think that's my goal in life – to never punch down. I'm all about fighting the power. Basically, I never want to hurt anyone. It's a big thing – being confident in your North Star. I know where my North Star is, and I know how to find it; that confidence gets me pretty far. When people start to muddy that, when they start worrying about the politics of their organisation rather than the actual cause, that's where the burnout happens. That's when everything can get diluted and you're not just punching the police, but each other. I've kind of just kept focused on who I was fighting – it has helped keep me on point.

Giedre Kubiliute: So, what's ahead? Obviously, you're saying it wouldn't happen in this day and age. What do you think things are going to be like in the future with, you know, the Police Bill and social media changing?

Jamie Klingler: Well, I applied for the London Policing Board, I got to the fourth round but I didn't get appointed, to be honest it feels like I swerved a bullet. But, really, I don't know what's next. I need to stop living crisis to crisis, from dead woman to dead woman. You don't want your adrenaline to spike and you don't want the times where you're most effective to be in the aftermath of a tragedy. I want be effective overall, not just to be a talking head when the next David Carrick or the next Wayne Couzens gets announced, because it is coming – we know it's coming. So I'm trying to figure out what the next strategies are for being effective, for being an agent of change, and I think that's the thing – there are little bits of progress.

But then there are big backslides and I need to figure out what is a way forward? Maybe that's as the head of purpose at an agency – that might be the next way to go. Is it to influence blue chip companies on how their language incorporates and is inclusive? I need to figure out where I fit. Where can I make the most impact and help the most people.

Ian R Lamond: Sad to say, I think we have run out of time. Thank you so much.

Giedre Kubiliute: Thank you, Jamie.

Jamie Klingler: No worries. Nice to speak to both of you.

Notes

1 Baroness Casey led an independent review into the culture and standards of behaviour in the Metropolitan Police. Its final report was released in March 2023. You can access the final report at: https://64e09bbc-abdd-42c6-90a8-58992ce46e59.usrfiles.com/ugd/64e09b_f3b0605584624bf5af-c024cd9d826e35.pdf
2 Rosa is a charity that campaigns for women's safety, health, and equality: https://rosauk.org/

References

Beck, G. (2010) *The Overton Window*. Threshold Editions.
Dufour, P. (2021) Comparing collective actions beyond national contexts: 'local spaces of protest' and the added value of critical geography. *Social Movement Studies*. 20 (2), 224–242.
Gøtzsche-Astrup, J. (2022) A sociological perspective on the experience of contention. *Sociological Theory*. 40 (3), 224–248.
Mouffe, C. & Laclau, E. (2014) *Hegemony and Socialist Strategy: Towards a Radical Democratic Politics*. Verso.
Mowatt, R.A. (2020) Events of dissent, events of the self: the liminality of protest images. In Lamond, I.R. & Moss, J. (eds) *Liminality and Critical Event Studies: Borders, Boundaries, and Contestation* (pp. 223–245). Springer.
Sabatier, P.A., & Weible, C.M. (2019) The advocacy coalition framework: innovations and clarifications. In Sabatier, P. (ed.) *Theories of the Policy Process*. Second Ed. (pp. 189–220). Routledge.
Santos, H. (2015) Social movements and lifeworld: making sense of subjective interpretation. In Oliveira, N., Hrubec, M., Sobottka, E. & Saavedra, G. (eds) *Justice and Recognition: On Axel Honneth and Critical Theory*.

https://filosofia.flu.cas.cz/upload/__ebook/ebook-383.pdf#page=400 Accessed: 31st October 2023.

Schumpeter, J. (2010) *Capitalism, Socialism, and Democracy.* Routledge Classics.

Teresa, G.C. (2022) Effects of mass media framing of protest movements: a meta-analysis and systematic review of mass media studies. *Online Journal of Communication and Media Technologies.* www.ojcmt.net/article/ effects-of-mass-media-framing-of-protest-movements-a-meta-analysis- and-systematic-review-of-mass-11538 Accessed: 9th November, 2023 DOI: https://doi.org/10.30935/ojcmt/11538

Index

Printed in the United States
by Baker & Taylor Publisher Services

Printed in the United States
by Baker & Taylor Publisher Services